THE BEAUTY COOKBOOK

THE BEAUTY COOKBOOK

*200 Recipes to Make Your Kitchen Your Spa
—for your face, your body, and your hair*

KYM DOUGLAS AND CINDY PEARLMAN

DUNHAM
BOOKS
Nashville

For information about bulk purchases or licensing of *The Beauty Cook-book*, please contact the publisher: Dunham Books, 63 Music Square East, Nashville, Tennessee 37203

Although the authors are experts in beauty trends, they are not trained medical professionals. The ideas and suggestions they offer in *The Beauty Cookbook* are not meant to be substituted for the medical advice of a physician. If you suffer from any allergy you should consult your doctor or trained medical professional before using any of the suggestions in this book. The authors and publisher disclaim any liability directly or indirectly from the use of this book.

Printed in the United States of America
ISBN 978-1-61623-576-5

Book and cover design and layout by Darlene Swanson
www.van-garde.com

dedication

We dedicate this book to
God's pharmacy and beauty shop.

CONTENTS

FOURTH COURSE *sexy body recipes* • *89*

Hot Chocolate Bath • Body Bubbly • Sexy, Soft Lips
Natural Breast Firmer • Margarita Salt Body Rub
Hot Legs • Sweet Body Bailout
Whipped Cream Body Extravaganza • Don't Sweat It (Anymore)
Chocolate Sexy Body Butter • Va Va Vanilla
Naked Ride Body Smoother • Take Two Aspirin
Go Directly to Glow • Strawberry Feet Forever
Hand It to Me • Vanilla Honey Tubbie

FIFTH COURSE *forty years young recipes* • *103*

E-I-E-I-O Facial • Brown Makes Us Frown • Puffy Eye RX
Make-a-Mohehill-out-of-a-Mountain Zit Zapper
Soy Hand Soak • Get-Rid-of-Wrinkles Secret Potion
Hot, Not So Much • Midnight Wanderer • Sun-kissed Smoothie
Tea, No Sympathy Facial • Tomato Face • Figs for Fine Lines

SIXTH COURSE *spa recipes* • *113*

Pina Colada Pampering
Margarita Salt Scrub with Punta Mita Tequila Massage
The Perfect Manicure Secret Trick • Cool-It Spa Compress
Quickie Exfoliator • Fast-Firming Face Masque • Aloe in Ice
Omega Me Masque • Hot Lips • Detoxing You from Head to Toe
Beauty Drinks Better Than a Cosmo
Health Benefits of Natural Juices & Broths • Skin Rejuvenator
Energy Regenerator • Cleansing Berry • Locks and the Key
Exfoliate Your Head—A Recipe for Oily Scalp Problems
BCB: Extra Helping

introduction

The following was inspired by actual events…

August, 2009. 6:58 p.m. on Rodeo Drive.
Otherwise known as Rock Bottom.

We skid into the valet section of the tony Neiman Marcus, tires burning rubber. A valet guy in black slacks and a starch white shirt says, "Where do you think you are, ladies? Compton?" Even though he looks like a male model from the current issue of GQ, we don't give his pecs a second glance, furiously lob him the keys, and break into a dead run. In heels, no less.

The heavy golden doors are closing, but the lock hasn't engaged. "Ladies, ladies, you can't…," screams the security guard.

To borrow a line from our new president, "Yes, we can!"

The store is officially closed and there isn't another patron anywhere, but there is a Dior dream at the end of the rainbow.

Winding past our old friends who have come through so many times in the past—Chanel, Clinique, and Estee (we love you)—we race to the counter with the giant navy-blue-and-gold

D above it. Almost reverently, we pause to pay respect to the spirit of Christian Dior. That's when the most disinterested saleslady in the world, her car keys in one hand and a package of cigarettes in the other, interrupts our reverie. (Smoking! Fine lines! Don't even get us started!)

"Miss, this is a virtual beauty emergency," Kym says. "Please help me! I need the Airflash Spray Foundation and the Skinflash Radiance Booster Pen—and I need it now."

"I'm so sorry, but the store is closed. The register is locked," Miss I-Don't–Care says.

Torn between arguing and running an index finger through a lovely late-summer-peach blush with a good SPF, Kym locks eyes with the woman in a gaze, reminiscent of Clint Eastwood during a shootout. Is Kym asking for the moon? No. She is just requesting a little understanding and the Diorshow Very Black mascara.

"Miss, I'm not asking you for the number 757 moisturizing lipstick. Just the foundation. Do you have these few additional items?" Kym whips out a list that looks like it was written to some cosmetics Santa.

Meanwhile, Cindy is busy gazing at the eye cream as if it's a BMW convertible. It might as well be because it costs about $100 for two dots of it. While dealing with her own beauty addiction, Cindy has been coveting high-end stores for months, living on samples of the eye cream and then begging for more, without ever buying anything. Is it stealing? Is it just exploratory moisturizing? Knowing her name must be on some "most-wanted lotion fugitive list" as a cosmetics sample con artist, Cindy was still harboring disappointment over a cosmetics lady in Scottsdale, Arizona, who, in the most stingy way, gave her a little glass vial with just two drops of the serum.

"I need more. What if I'm allergic? I need to try it for maybe two weeks," Cindy said.

"You're not lathering your entire body with it," said the knowing cosmetics lady. "Two drops is enough to try it. For one day."

Nothing like a cosmetics woman who is onto your game.

7:05 PM. NEIMAN MARCUS IN BEVERLY HILLS. THE NEW LOW.

Kym runs with five new Dior items to several cosmetics counters, and no register is open. "We might need to take those back and you'll have to come back tomorrow," says the cosmetics woman who thinks she might pry the items out of Kym's hand. Peace in the Middle East is more likely tonight.

"Certainly, there is still a register open somewhere?" Kym begs, holding her products in a death grip. "What about in shoes? There must be some old lady who is still thinking about $700 flip flops."

"Can I have a sample of eye cream?" Cindy interrupts to beg the woman for her fix.

"I don't have any vials," Miss-I'm-Getting-Mad-Now counters.

"I have my own vial. In my purse," Cindy says.

"Take as much as you want," the woman says with a dismissive tone.

"God, why didn't I bring a shampoo bottle?" Cindy whispers to Kym as she wonders if drinking the stuff right from the sample tube might work just as well.

INTERVENTION!

Hello, we're Kym and Cindy, and you might know us from our best selling beauty books, *The Black Book of Hollywood Beauty Secrets*, *The Black Book of Hollywood Diet Secrets*, and *The Black Book of Hollywood Pregnancy Secrets*. Or, you may know us from Kym's appearances on the top-rated daytime talk show *Ellen*. Now we have a confession: *We're beauty addicts who truly needed to start our own support group called Cosmetics Anonymous.*

That night at Neiman Marcus was when we realized we needed an intervention, and it wasn't just about cosmetics, but for all beauty items from moisturizers to body scrubs to hair masks. We almost got locked in the Beverly Hills style Mecca overnight, which honestly wouldn't have been such a bad thing. Even months later, Kym muses, "Why did I need that spray foundation? Where was I going? The red carpet? No. Dinner out? No. Why did I need to have it right then? But I did."

Is there a woman on this planet who doesn't understand?

Cindy, who has a stockpile now of free eye cream, and doesn't even really have dark circles or wrinkles to begin with, nodded her head because her bathroom actually looks like a high-end cosmetic counter. She has had a series of short-lived, unfulfilling relationships with past loves that weren't really honest and forthright when it came to keeping their promises. They went by names like Kiehls and Nars—and, by the way, Burt, you can keep your bees to yourself forever more.

Yes, we realized that we were in serious trouble.

And we staged our own intervention.

Now we're under house arrest in the best way possible, although there are no stylish ankle bracelets to keep us at home. Instead, we have blenders, mixing bowls, and a whisk attached to our wrists.

These days, we get our beauty fixes from our own kitchens. Yes, our *kitchens*. We're still on a beauty high, but with products we create from our own homes.

We cook beauty—all natural, whole, fresh, and very affordable, head-to-toe beauty with supplies you can find in your kitchen. When we say "fresh face," we mean *really, really fresh*.

What we offer you in *The Beauty Cookbook* is a way to look

absolutely gorgeous, while breaking your addiction to the high-end (and costly) beauty world. You can save thousands of dollars by using beauty products you can find in your own home or make from a few simple and all-natural ingredients that are probably on your shelves right now. We culled from our team of beauty experts hundreds of pure, good-for-you, great-for-your-skin, hair and body recipes that actually contain the same ingredients as the high-end products: green tea, milk, olive oil, almond oil, sugars, baking soda, and other common products in your pantry or cupboard. Why are you paying so much for what you already have in your cabinets? Ketchup as a hair color correction or a margarita body scrub.

Pass the tequila and read on.

We've broken it down to the core, active ingredients that cost pennies to use. When you buy high-end items, you're buying the same ingredients in this book and a ton of useless lotion. Our beauty team agrees that products you can make at home in the freshest way possible are actually better than anything you could ever buy at the store. And many of our celebrity friends and clients also agree with us!

Our quest to look younger, prettier, and our most gorgeous selves will never end. But now we are the ones in control, and we're not harassing poor salesladies at closing time. They can keep their eye creams to themselves. This book will show you how to make a better one.

What we needed that night at Neiman's is what you have in your hands right now—this book.

Welcome to *The Beauty Cookbook*.

how to use this book. . .and why

It would be nice to say that we were the first ladies to come up with the idea of kitchen beauty recipes, but our crack team of researchers at Beauty Cookbook Headquarters (BCB HQ) found out that there were some gals in the 16th century who beat us to this idea. Don't you hate it when that happens? What were they trying to do? Get a deal with Oprah?

BUT WE DIGRESS.

Back in the day—way, way back—women didn't smell as good (but hey, neither did the men), and they still wanted to look gorgeous. Of course, they couldn't run out to the local Wal-Mart for these products, or even a high-end mall, so they were stuck with what was right at their lovely fingertips, including milk, cream, oils, and even eggs, grapes and lemons.

Time moved on, as it always seems to do, and then came Nostradamus, who helped out the ladies when it came to natural beauty recipes. He was the first alchemist to turn herbs and flowers into spa treatments in the days when they didn't even have spas that charged $150 for putting a few cucumbers on your eyes and scrubbing your body down with what really is just $1 worth of Kosher salt. Nostradamus decided to take his beauty recipes and write them down into what eventually became a much sought-after book, or dare we say the first beauty best-seller.

With great humbleness and pride, we want to follow in the gorgeous footsteps of some of our ancient beauty cooks to bring you the timeless secrets that have kept women looking fabulous over the ages.

This brings us to the part of this book where we help you figure out what to do and how much to do. The answer really is simple: Do a little or do a lot. Try a few recipes, or try them all based on your skin, your hair types, and your lifestyle. Some recipes might work better for your skin type and others might make the PTA mom next to you at the bake sale really glow. Don't hate her because she's dutiful about putting green tea on her face. Your glow might come from soy. As they say, variety is the spice of life—and of a great beauty regime.

We would like to suggest that you don't just work on your skin, although there are more skin recipes in this book than anything else, because our readers have demanded them as an alternative to shots, cutting, or lifting, oh my. There are some amazing hair treatments that will help even the most impossible locks. Page through your book and find softening, firming, and de-aging recipes that will cover you (literally) from head to toe. Mark what you love the best so you can remember to add it to your regular regime and stage some "do-overs."

This book is also peppered with quick beauty tips. These will add one more layer of beauty know-how to your routine with time-tested and quick ways to look more gorgeous. You don't have to try them with the recipes, but it's a good idea to go the extra step to look and feel great. We will also offer a few fun asides that reveal our worst beauty nightmares and how we fixed them.

The point of *The Beauty Cookbook* is to boost your self-confidence, because the only one you truly need to feel pretty for in this life is yourself. We hope these recipes make you feel gorgeous both inside and out.

We leave you with our BFF Cleopatra—a head-strong woman who knew a thing or two about being a major hottie of her day. Cleo, it turns out, could have shared soy lattes with us because she endorsed looking great with homemade products. There was Cleo ordering around her peasant ladies and demanding they go to the local market to find her some hydroxy acids that would help her legendary skin glow. When the sun went down, she dunked her body in milk, knowing that she wanted to smell better and feel soft for Mark Anthony. She also knew that milk had lactic acid in it, which is the most effective alpha hydroxy. By the way, in the 1990s, cosmetic company geniuses figured out Cleo's secret and started selling it to you for big bucks after they put the exact same ingredients Cleo used in their skincare lotions and cleansers.

Cleo, we bow to your resourcefulness.

Now, it's our turn to get cooking…and turn up the heat.

FIRST COURSE *facial recipes*

love you, honey face wash

Sugar? We prefer to sing, "Honey, honey…." We found a great reason to go to a natural or health food store, and now you're going to create a very inexpensive and quite natural cleanser that will replace bar soap in your house while making your skin clean and moisturized at the same time. Remember that we never soap up in our kitchen (or bathroom), but only use cleanser. When you create one that is gentle and gives you a moisture boost, then it's a win-win beauty situation. Please *do try* this at home, but pay close attention to the fact that this must be refrigerated after you use it. Before you put it in the fridge the first time,

Beauty Tip
Don't hate your favorite
film star because her face
always looks so impossibly
dewy-fresh all the time. Yes,
she just spent two hours in
a makeup chair on a set,
but you can do it yourself
at home. To wit: Get dewy
in your own bathroom by
filling up your sink with
steaming hot water. Step
away from the heat. Now,
put on your makeup. When
you are done, stick your face
into the lingering steam
and count to five. Viola!
Suddenly, all that moisture
that you just layered on will
make you look as dewy and
glowing as a movie star.

remember to mark it as a beauty product and not a yummy ice-cream topping!

¼   cup raw honey (usually found at Whole Foods or health food stores)
1   tablespoon of liquid soap
½   cup glycerin (found at beauty stores or even at a drug store)
1   sticker
     A clean plastic bottle

Mix the honey, soap, and glycerin in a small bowl. Dunk a wash-cloth in warm water and pour a large dollop of this mixture into the cloth. Wash your face with the wet washcloth and then gently dry it. Your face will feel clean from the soap, and soft and mois-turized from the honey, which is extremely good for you because it contains several antioxidants and also has an antiseptic quality. Take the remaining mixture and pour it into the plastic bottle. Here's the twist: This must be refrigerated between uses, and we don't want your hubby pouring soapy honey on his toast in the morning and saying, "Honey, I love this...can you make me more of this tasty treat...but wait, my stomach is doing cartwheels." You must put a big sticker on your bottle. We like to write: BCB CLEANSER. DO NOT EAT THIS UNDER THE PENALTY OF THE BEAUTY POLICE (Mom).

peachy clean

2   pitted peaches
1   tablespoon olive oil
     brown sugar (use as little or as much as you want to exfoli-ate)

Puree the peaches in your blender or food processor. Transfer the contents to a bowl, add the olive oil and as much brown sugar as you want to create a scrub. If you have sensitive skin, use less sugar for less abrasion. You can use this mixture as an entire body scrub. The natural vitamin C in the peaches will also serve as a skin brightener, and will result in the same glow that you get after your standard $100 facial at the spa.

we feel like cuke-ing

Your favorite eye cream that has caffeine in it (check the ingredients)

A few slices of fresh cucumber

Okay, you pulled an all-nighter with your significant other or enjoyed a night out with your girlfriends. You look like death-warmed-over on only two hours sleep. And to make matters worse, it's 100 percent guaranteed that from the pizza and that bottle of red wine you will be puffy—the not-so-magic mama in the morning.

It's your BCB gals to the rescue! All you need is to keep a good cream on hand that has some caffeine in it (anti-wrinkle creams usually do). When you wake up puffy, slather the cream under your eyes, on the side of your nose, and up and down your jaw line. Now, run to the fridge and rip those cuke slices off tonight's salad

Beauty Tip

In a hurry and want to look like you just stepped out of the most expensive facial at your local spa? No worries. Just grab a fresh peach. Get rid of the skin and mash the pulp in a bowl with a fork. Transfer the mixture to your gorgeous face. Rest for 10 minutes, and don't walk around. (We're not responsible for peach pulp on your pricey couch if you can't sit still.) The vitamin C in the peaches will act as a stunning skin brightener. After ten minutes, rinse your face and you're ready to glow.

because this is a beauty 911 moment. Of course, you can cut up a few fresh slices.

Return to the bathroom looking like you're having a healthy snack. The reality is, you will take those nice cold cuke slices and rub them on your face and over the cream in tiny circular motions. You need to keep circling upwards and to the side, think up, up, and away. Do this for about two minutes, and watch the puffiness go down, because the caffeine is bringing the water retention in your face down, while the natural astringent in the cuke is also killing the swelling. Now, pass us a piece of that leftover pizza as a big thank you.

you say tomato, i say tomat-o

It was a long night with a few too many cocktails, salty foods, and a bedtime that neared 3 AM. You can force yourself out of bed in the morning, but your skin will still look like it wants to be flattened to your pillow because it's in the beauty Witness Protection Program. Here's a quick pick-me-up recipe that will make it look like you stayed in last night, did a little laundry, and then called your grandmother. Only we know the truth.

1　**tomato cut into thin slices**
2　**teaspoons of lemon juice**
　　A pinch of baking soda

Cut two thin tomato slices and rub them all over your face. When you're done, discard them—oh, so-not appetizing in to-night's salad now—and mix in a small bowl the lemon juice and baking soda. Take this "paste" and coat your face with it. Give it 20 minutes to really sink in and then wash it off until you don't feel any of the grit from the baking soda. Your skin will suddenly have the glow of a $200 facial.

after-dinner drink

Dinner is over and you are (finally) finished with the dishes. Here's a little tip on how to keep your skin looking and feeling great: Just grab a bottle of almond oil from the kitchen and bring it into the bathroom. Instead of slathering on that chemical, fragrance-additive and paraben-filled lotion on your skin after your shower, just rub the almond oil on your elbows, knees, and the bottom of your feet *before* you shower. You will be creating a thin shield that will keep your skin from drying out due to the hot water.

saturday-morning sugar scrub

You've had your breakfast, so now it's time to feed your skin.

1   cup sugar
½   cup sweet almond oil
4   natural-source vitamin E capsules
12 drops essential oil of neroli

Pierce and drain the vitamin E into a plastic bowl, discarding the capsules. Add remaining ingredients and, once in the shower, mix well by hand. Working from the neck down, massage generous scoops into the shoulders, arms, and torso, paying extra attention to neglected areas on the upper back. Sugarcoat your derriere, thighs, knees, and shins, using any extra scrub on the rough skin on your ankles and heels. Hug yourself to make sure you've scrubbed the dead cells off every inch of your torso and limbs, and inhale: aroma therapists say neroli is calming. Rinse off with care (floor will be slippery) and pat your skin dry with a towel. No need to moisturize, as you'll know from your glow.

tin woman

Forget gold and silver. To look beautiful, all you need is a little bit of tin.

If your face is feeling puffy, just reach for the tinfoil. Take a face-side piece of tinfoil, rip it off, and put it in the freezer for 20 minutes. Place it on your face and cut out a small hole for your mouth so you can breathe! Next, mold the foil to your face and leave it there for about ten minutes. It's a cheap way to create your own face-cooling mask and decrease all inflammation. Celeb makeup artist Ramy Gafni uses this treatment on Britney Spears before she goes on stage—and it only costs pennies!

hollywood magic moisture mask

In Hollywood, there are several places that all the celebrities go to when they have a Red Carpet event and they just have to look fabulous. One of our favorite picks is the Sonya Dakar Skin Clinic in Beverly Hills. This is the first of many recipes Sonya has shared with *The Beauty Cookbook*, from her secret file. Of course, we only chose the ones she gives her most famous A-list clients to try at home.

Beauty Tip

Here's a great way to save from buying moisturizer all of the time. Just cut your application of cream down by one-fourth. Most women just glob it on, when the truth is your entire face can be covered by cream the size of one kernel of corn. The trick is to make sure to moisturize damp skin so that the moisturizer sinks into your pores, and you will also use less. You will even have enough for your neck if it's damp. Now, if you could only stop your mate from glopping on your cream. One woman we know told her husband that her moisturizer had female hormones in it. A tiny white lie, but he stayed on his half of the bathroom forever after that little revelation.

This is one of Sonya's best homemade masks that serves as a perfect dry skin fix, because it has hydrating and soothing ingredients including aloe vera gel and honey.

½ medium-sized avocado, peeled and pitted
2 tablespoons aloe vera gel
1 tablespoon honey
2 tablespoon oatmeal (not instant)
1 teaspoon grapeseed oil (available at grocery and health food stores)

Using a fork, mash the avocado in the bowl until it is semismooth, but still has a few lumps. Add the aloe vera gel to the avocado and mix together thoroughly. Add the rest of the ingredients and stir until totally blended.

Wash face and pat dry. Scoop out a small handful of the mask and smear it on your face. Apply till you have covered the skin, avoiding the delicate area around the eyes.

Relax for 15 minutes while the mask absorbs into the face. Rinse with warm water and pat dry.

MORE OF SONYA DAKAR'S STELLAR AT-HOME SKIN RECIPES

chocolate crème (sonya dakar chocolate ultima power shake)

2 heaping tablespoons of silken tofu
1 cup soy milk, plain or vanilla
4-8 ice cubes
1 teaspoon of flax seeds
¼ cup of strawberries and/or blueberries

Blend all of the above in your blender for one minute and serve immediately! The soy protein is great for your skin, as are the Omega-3 rich flax seeds, which help to hydrate your skin. Adding the antioxidant rich berries gives you the perfect detox!

sonya dakar's antioxidant exfoliating face cleanser for dry or dehydrated skin

1   oz. rapeseed oil
1   teaspoon of ground flax seeds
½   teaspoon of chamomile tea (from a cooled and steeped tea bag)

Blend all of the ingredients well in a blender or in a bowl with a whisk. Massage it into your wet skin. Then wipe it off with a warm towel. The rapeseed oil is high in anti-oxidants, while the Omega-3-rich flax seeds gently exfoliate. The chamomile is an extra boost for calming sensitive skin.

look-younger face liquid

In this economy, who can afford to go to the dermatologist anymore for those monthly pick-me-ups? Not us. For years, women have been literally running to the docs to get alpha-hydroxy products and peels for their highly touted exfoliating, peeling, and smoothing ef-

Beauty Tip
You're on the self-improvement bandwagon, so why not have a spicy snack with a little bit of Tabasco sauce on it, or add red peppers to a salad. Both will raise your metabolism and help keep your appetite in check. A study of people who ate foods with red peppers consumed far fewer calories during the day and even boosted their metabolism by 25 percent.

fects on the complexion. These professional peels work, but they are very pricey.

We found a fabulous homemade face liquid that will do wonders for your skin, and all the ingredients are probably in your kitchen already! This recipe comes to us from aromatherapist, natural health-expert and author, Julia Meadows, who wrote *Natural Body Care*.

In it, she reveals that recent studies have shown that the epidermis is able to absorb vitamins and nutrients from topically applied liquid juice solutions, greatly benefiting the strength, elasticity, and general appearance of the skin.

A juicer is best, but you can also make this by freshly squeezing the ingredients.

1	**large, peeled grapefruit, or a small bottle of fresh-squeezed grapefruit juice**
1	**large, green apple, peeled and cored, or a small bottle of fresh-squeezed apple juice**
1	**large, ripe tomato, or bottle of tomato juice**
½	**teaspoon of grapefruit-seed extract**

Beauty Tip

Here is an instant acid peel. Blend 1 tablespoon of orange juice and 1 tablespoon of lemon juice with a cup of yogurt. Apply it to your face and keep it on for 15 minutes. Then rinse or wipe it off with a wet face towel.

Pass all pieces through an electric juicer or mix bottled juices together. Add grapefruit-seed extract. Pour into glass bottle and refrigerate until using. Saturate cotton balls and apply over face and neck, avoiding the eyes and lips. Keep on face for 15 minutes. Rinse with cool water.

you-don't-bring-me-flowers facial

1   **packet of crushed rose petals (or use the petals from your
    roses after they're dried out)**
    **Essential oil of your choice from a health or natural food
    store**

Crush the rose petals until they are in small flakes. You can crush
them to virtually powder-sized flakes if you have small pores.
The rule is, the bigger your pores, the bigger the flakes. Mix
the petals with a tablespoon of an essential oil of your choice. A
wonderful one to purchase is natural tangerine oil, which can be
found at some grocery stores. Use this as both a face and body
scrub. Your entire body will smell like a bouquet of roses. You can
save the rest of the dried crushed petals for another treatment.

coconut facial

¼   **cup of shredded coconut shards**
    **Essential oil of your choice from a health or natural food
    store**

If you can't afford an island vacation these days, you can still
smell like you just returned from one. Mix three tablespoons of
essential oil with the ¼ cup of coconut pieces. Rub all over your
face, arms, and legs as a wonderful full-body exfoliant. The oil
in the coconut will smooth your skin, while removing dead skin
and makeup. An added benefit is that the smell lingers, and for
at least another 24 hours you will have a hint of a coconut smell
that makes everyone around you crave a pina colada...or a tropical kiss.

dry skin smoothie

1   **banana**
1   **cup of yogurt**
1   **tablespoon of honey**
2   **tablespoons rolled oats**

Purée the banana and then add yogurt, honey, and oats. Blend well. Smooth the mixture over your damp skin. Let it sink in for 15 minutes and then rinse. Your face will be instantly hydrated.

red skin smoothie

3½   **ounces brewed rose hip tea**
3½   **ounces chamomile tea**
2   **ounces aloe vera juice**

Brew the tea and let cool to room temperature. Shake all the liquids together in a martini shaker or pitcher. Pour the liquid into a misting bottle. Wash your face with your regular cleanser and then mist your face with this treatment. Mist twice a day to decrease the redness.

lemon light

To brighten a dull complexion, do this lemon juice mask, which will also help whisk away dead cells from the surface of your skin.

1   **cup of mashed seedless grapes**
1   **tablespoon of whole-wheat flour**
1   **teaspoon of lemon juice**

Beauty Tip

If your oily skin produces adult acne, you can make a quick home fix by simply putting a dab of white toothpaste on your pimples. If you do this in the morning, the zit will be dry by the end of the day and gone the next day.

Mix ingredients. Paint the mixture onto your face with a small, clean paintbrush. Leave on for 20 minutes and rinse off with warm water, followed by a rinse with cool water. Turn down the lights. You are too bright and beautiful!

oil not-so-slick facial

We feel for the ladies who deal with oil slicks every single day when they look in the mirror at their shining faces. (Remember when Michelle Pfeiffer in *Hairspray* gave her daughter a horrified glance and shrieked, "Shiny!") For some reason, your non-teenage skin still produces ample amounts of oil, and you always feel a bit greasy or shiny. There are a few tricks to deal with oily skin, including washing your face fewer times a day. The more you wash, the more you will stimulate oil production. You can also try this drying home facial.

1   **egg white**
½   **cup strawberries**

Mix the egg white and the strawberries together. Apply to your face and allow at least 10 minutes for it to penetrate. The protein in the egg while will tighten your face, while the tart strawberries will act as a natural astringent.

lemon head

We know that lemons are a great way to treat blemishes, but they're also a secret weapon if you're unhappy with your skin tone. We're not advocating bleaching out your skin with lemons, but if your skin tone is uneven, you can correct the problem with this simple recipe that will even things out.

½   cup fresh lemon juice
3   tablespoons Witch Hazel
1   small plastic bottle

Place the above ingredients in a small plastic bottle and shake well. Simply take this mixture and put it on a washrag or cotton ball.

Lightly go over your entire face to even out your skin tone. Do this several times over a week until you're happy with the results. (Thanks to Janice Cox from her book *EcoBeauty*.)

Beauty Tip
If you're prone to dry skin, then follow this rule each time you wash your face. Make sure to wash, and then quickly pat your skin, but don't get rid of all the water. Put on your moisturizer by using that little bit of water to make it spread evenly while the water on your face acts as a secondary hydration treatment. You can practice this on your entire body by dabbing yourself dry with a towel and then applying a little oil or moisturizer to your entire face, which is slightly damp.

Beauty Tip

This is for you smokers out there. Please get those butts out of your life. There is absolutely nothing good about lighting up. We're not going to get into the damage you're doing to your lungs and other body organs. This is a beauty book, so the focus is your skin. A top dermatologist tells us that smokers rapidly age their skin because the smoke results in sulfuric acid hitting your surface skin cells. It also penetrates deeply to the point that facialists tell us the minute they remove the dead skin they can immediately smell old smoke. There is no product or home cure to stop the lines and wrinkles or the dead-looking, old skin that smoking produces. By the way, the nicotine in cigarettes also constricts the blood vessels on your face and turns your skin gray. The acetaldehyde in cigarettes actually goes after the fibers that hold younger looking skin together, while the chemicals in those cigarettes start attacking the collagen that keeps your skin looking plump and young. Another side effect of puffing away is that your lips will suddenly form zillions of fine lines, as will the skin around your mouth. You will age your face a decade beyond your biological age if you continue to smoke. Our advice: Kick the habit for good. If your health isn't enough of a reason, then quit for vanity. Just quit.

---

just-you-honey facial

For those who like to keep it simple, you can't get more basic than a one-ingredient facial. Anyone—and we mean anyone—has the time to do this quick fix that yields major skin results.

2   tablespoons of pure or organic honey

Wash your face with cleanser and warm water. Now that you're super clean and ready, just take those two tablespoons of honey and rub them over your entire mug (but don't get it in your eyes).

Leave this pure honey mask on for ten minutes and then

rinse it off. The honey will keep your pores super tight while smoothing your skin and leaving it with a natural glow. Honey works because it's a natural humectant that keeps the moisture sealed inside.

So, bee grateful to our little insect friends who are like nature's Oil of Olay.

no *fluff de-puff*

You had a private "screening" of the *Sex and the City* movie at home and invited your own personal Carrie, Miranda, Samantha, and Charlotte. Someone brought a couple of bottles of wine and a bag of tortilla chips, plus that amazing homemade guacamole dip. Somehow, as you were coveting their skinny-mini Prada dresses, you drank three glasses of wine and ate several handfuls of salty chips. The worst thing is, your eyes are going to be extra puffy in the morning.

Beauty Tip

Whiten and brighten your face fast with a simple tip. Rub a raw potato on your face to remove spots and pigments.

We're not here to deal with hangover or carb overloading, but we do know how to get rid of the puff. Before you go to bed at night—and even if you don't feel like it and just want to flop into your bed and skip beauty regimes—you must drink two (not one, but two) eight-ounce glasses of water. Immediately afterwards, find your thickest eye cream and put it on liberally before you fall into bed. The water will get rid of the fluids, which is key here, because booze plus salt causes your entire body to retain liquids, and some of it goes to your eye area. The lotion will also help bring down any "pillows" that dare to crop up during the wee hours.

cheerios facial scrub

The kids are home from school and all they want to eat is Cheerios. It's healthy and fun to eat, but you need a little mommy time and a pick-me-up. Just grab the kids' Cheerios. You'll be looking refreshed, renewed, and glowing in minutes with this all-American favorite beauty trick. The Cheerios are made from oats, which help to rid the skin of dead dry cells. The lemon juice contains citric acid, which helps to brighten the skin and kills bacteria on the surface of the face, and the honey is a natural moisturizer. Combined, they are a beauty tip fit for a hero!

1   **handful of Cheerios cereal**
1   **teaspoon of honey**
    A few drops of real lemon juice

Throw a handful of Cheerios in the blender. Blend until a fine powder.

In a bowl, mix powdered Cheerios with the honey. Add the drops of lemon juice to the mixture. Apply the thick sticky paste to the face. Sit for 10 minutes. Rinse with warm water.

shhhh... star secret

Scarlett Johansson tells us that when she wakes up with a zit (yes, it actually happens…alert the CNN crawl!), she reaches into her freezer for relief. "If it's a swollen blemish or my eyes are puffy, I use whatever's in my freezer. I'll rest a bag of frozen blueberries on my eyes. It's not uncommon to see me before a premiere with a bottle of Ketel One stuck to my eyelid."

the english rose beauty scrub

Across the pond in jolly old London, the weather is often drab, rainy, and cold. No wonder those ladies stop for a spot of tea and a scone. All that damp weather and chill factor could leave an English rose feeling a tad bit wilted from the weight of dry or dead skin cells. Here's a quick Brit fix to make your skin feel silky, smooth, and fresh. We recommend trying this on your body and not your face because the salt is a little too harsh for queens, princesses, or even regular old American women.

½   **cup of sea salt or Kosher salt**
2   **teaspoons of coconut oil**
1   **teaspoon of fresh, chopped mint**
    Zest from one lemon

In a small bowl, mix the coconut oil, mint and lemon zest (which you will grate from a fresh lemon). Add the Kosher salt and lightly toss until the liquid is covering the salt. Bring the scrub into the tub or shower with you. Think good Bridget Jones thoughts as you scrub away the daily stress and dead skin cells.

Cheerio, ladies! Now, if only Hugh Grant or Clive Owen could feel your skin this smooth.

tea for you

A flushed face might signal that you're blushing from a happy surprise...or, the fact that your face is constantly a little reddish and you hate that heinous fact of life. A quick fix is to just grab a tea bag, dunk it in cool water, and then place it on those red areas. This quick fix causes the blood vessels to constrict and move away from the surface area of your skin. Suddenly, the red is gone, and you're back to looking normal and blush-free. The tea is also good on sunburned areas of your body for quick pain relief. Just leave the tea bags on for 15 minutes. The tannins in the tea will calm swelling and ease tender areas because they contain a natural astringent.

tea for you 2

It's the end of the month when that pesky mortgage needs to be paid—not to mention the electricity bill and the cable. You can't really afford to run in for a $100 facial, but you need something to take the set of luggage bags out from under your eyes. This works every single time, and only it costs pennies.

2   bags of black or green tea.
Warm water

Simply moisten both tea bags until they're wet, but not dripping. Get in a comfortable position where you're reclining in a chair, a couch, or a bed.

Place one bag on the swollen area. Relax for 10 whole minutes, and that means no funny stuff like taking care of the kids or making dinner.

This works because tea is full of more caffeine than coffee, and caffeine naturally reduces swelling by reducing surface blood vessels. The tea is a natural skin tightener, too. If you use green tea, it will also help to get rid of the pain of sunburn. Green tea is an antioxidant that has been known to protect you from skin cancer.

This is a great treatment if you have a big dinner out with your significant other, or if you stayed out a little bit too late the night before. Just remember that you don't want the tea bags to be steaming hot or you will burn your skin. They should feel cool, and make sure you keep your eyes closed during the treatment. Put on a little bit of music and de-stress. Your entire body will thank you for that 10-minute reprieve from daily life.

tea for you 3

It seems only natural to do an IV drip of Starbucks in the morning, but we have a suggestion that's for your health, your diet, and to get your skin glowing. Try to sip some white tea, because each cup is chock-full of 50 mg of L-thenine, a natural mental booster that will wake up your mind without giving you a jittery rush. Some 20–30 minutes after your first few sips and you will feel like you just took a cold shower. This works because L-thenine activates your alpha brain waves, making your mind more active while retaining a calm state. We know that you'll just hate the news that the white tealeaf blocks the production of new fat cells in your body and even helps to break down stubborn fat that's been plaguing you. Can we all jump into a vat of white tea?

Beauty Tip
If you put on slow music during eating you will eat 25 percent less during each meal. A study at John Hopkins University indicates that people who listen to slow music while eating actually time their bites to the music, eat slower, and fill up much faster! Pretty cool, huh?

FOOD FOR THE SKIN

We here at Beauty Cookbook Headquarters scour the globe and the refrigerator for ideas, tricks, and concoctions that will make you look your best for less, while keeping it all-natural and wholesome. However, we all know that what we put in our bodies is as important as what we put on them! So, we bow our heads to Dr. Leilie Javen, a certified plastic surgeon who specializes in cosmetic procedures. The good doctor says, "If your diet is missing certain nutrients, your skin will look dry, sallow, and old." These were fighting words, so we have to fix this situation right now!

The good doc says there are six top foods you should put in your grocery cart to ensure great skin from the inside out:

1. Flaxseed: Well-known for its heart-healthy Omega-3, this oil keeps your skin healthy and protects skin from reddening, roughness and scaling, while helping it stay hydrated.

2. Pomegranates: This exotic super food is loaded with antioxidants, which boast anti-aging and sun protective properties. It also has collagen-boosting properties.

3. Green, leafy vegetables and spinach: These Garden-of-the-God treats contain lutein and beta-carotene. Lutein protects the skin from sun damage, while keeping it hydrated and increases elasticity.

4. Tomato Sauce/Paste: Rich in lycopene, this gives tomatoes their bright red pigment and helps neutralize UV light's damaging effects.

Beauty Tip

You're not supposed to bake in the sun, but you threw caution to the wind on your vacation in Florida or the French Riviera. Now, you look like a cross between a lobster and the red crayon in your child's coloring book. It turns out that aloe vera is still one of the best remedies. We suggest keeping your aloe vera gel in the fridge to enjoy both the hydrating and healing of the product, while getting a nice chill on your hot spots. You can also grow an aloe vera plant in your kitchen and pick off the leaves. Simply squeeze out the liquid inside and you can apply it directly to your sunburn.

5. Dark Chocolate: Chock-full of flavanols, this keeps the skin soft, smooth, strong and hydrated.

6. Green Tea and Berries: This is a favorite for gorgeous skin, thanks to their high antioxidant content. "Fresh brewed green tea, as well as strawberries, raspberries, blueberries, and blackberries have anti-inflammatory properties and reduce the aging effects," says Dr. Javan.

you pumpkin face

We love the fall season because the colors change, the air gets a bit nippy in the most wonderful way, and there's a wealth of products that work wonders on the face and body. Around Halloween time, make sure you keep the goop you scoop out of your pumpkin because it makes an amazing facial! Pumpkin is loaded with beta carotene, and your skin will love it. (Plus, we hate to see you spend big money on pumpkin spa treatments or pumpkin exfoliating masks that are basically just pumpkin puree with some nice lady slathering it on you while Enya plays in the background.) You can achieve the same results at home with a mask that will help improve your skin texture and correct damage, while smoothing and soothing. There's nothing scary about that plan for Halloween.

¾ cup of pureed pumpkin

Take the innards of the pumpkin, mash it up or pop into your food processor until it's pulpy, but not a liquid.

Smooth the puree onto your face and leave on for 10 minutes. Rinse off.

soy-milking it

It's Saturday morning and you wake up around 10ish. The paper is on the driveway, someone walked the dog (thank goodness for teenagers who want to drive the family car), and you just want to stay in your robe with a soy latte magically appearing out of nowhere. Speaking of soy, you should also do a little facial after you read the show biz section. Soymilk, when combined with a bit of barley malt, is a great home recipe to moisturize your skin, cleanse your pores, and tighten your face. Edensoy has a great firming facial.

Beauty Tip

We've finally found a good use for mayonnaise and it won't go to your bum. Take 2 tablespoons of full-fat mayo and apply to your face. Let it sink in for 10 minutes and then wash. Your face will feel tight and soft because mayo contains vitamin A to get rid of dead skin cells and the fat in it helps moisturize and keep your skin smooth.

¼   cup unsweetened Edensoy Original
1½   teaspoons Eden Organic Barley Malt Syrup

Combine the Edensoy and barley malt in a cup and mix thoroughly. Leave on for 10 minutes. Wash the mixture off with warm water. Your skin will feel clean and fresh and you'll look wonderful.

THE BUDDHA NOSE KNOWS RECIPES

We love our friends at the Buddha Nose in California. They believe in organic mind/body beauty. The company (www.buddhanose.com) is a certified organic body-care brand that focuses on how inner balance affects outer balance. They also believe that beauty equals simplicity and focus on nature-centered, sustainable practices, while enjoying a healthy lifestyle.

"Beauty is about feeling good, and Buddha Nose understands that the simple act of doing something good for ourselves makes us feel beautiful," says Buddha Nose founder Amy Galper, who was a New York City-based shiatsu practitioner. Amy has also created handmade beauty products in her kitchen, which makes her a soul sister to us.

By the way, all of their products are totally free of all synthetics and chemical preservative systems. "The skin is our largest organ, and by using only organic ingredients, we not only respect the health and well-being of our bodies, but we also respect the health and well-being of our environment," Amy says.

These are her favorite recipes. Thanks, Amy!

simple dark honey facial

2   tablespoons very dark honey

Gently warm 2 tablespoons of very dark honey. Apply all over face, making sure the honey is not too warm. Let it stay on your face for 15 minutes. Rinse with warm, and cool water alternately. Pat dry.

sugar scrub with green tea and fresh ginger (for the body)

1   cup of organic sugar
2   tablespoons of fresh, grated ginger root
1   cup of lukewarm green tea

Brew one strong cup of green tea. Let it sit and cool until lukewarm.

Grate two tablespoons of fresh ginger. Mix all ingredients into a bowl. Use immediately as a body scrub in your bath or shower before the sugar dissolves.

oatmeal cucumber mint facial cleanser

¼   **cup of cooked organic oatmeal**
2   **fresh organic mint leaves**
2   **tablespoons of peeled, seeded, and chopped organic cucumber**

Mix all ingredients in a small food processor until puréed. Use as a facial cleanser and rinse with warm water.

prune face

That old saying, "You old prune face," could not be further from the truth. In actuality Prunes are great for your face and your digestion. Eat them, purée them, and put them on your face, but anyway you look at it, prunes are good for you. They are full of fiber and can promote a healthy digestive tract. Prunes also keep the skin healthy and rid your body of toxins.

kimberly king's exfoliating and hydrating avocado delight facial scrub

1   **avocado (ripe)**
1   **teaspoon of cornmeal**
     Your favorite pure essential oil (a few drops)
     Jojoba oil (a few drops)

Avocado Delight should be applied on freshly cleansed skin, removing all traces of makeup. It should also be made fresh and used fresh on skin. Do not store in the refrigerator and use at a later time.

By hand (with a fork or spoon), mix only ½ an avocado in a bowl until all the chunks are gone. It should be a paste-like consistency. After mixing the avocado, blend in one teaspoon of cornmeal, slowly stirring to keep the consistency smooth. Add just a few drops of jojoba oil and mix. There should not be too much oil added to the mix because you don't want the ingredients to liquefy.

If you find the scrub is too dry for your skin, carefully add a drop or two of pure essential oil and then mix. Make sure you can smell the essential oil in the mix. Some recommended essential oils are lavender, vanilla, eucalyptus, rosewood, bergamot, lemon, ylang ylang, cedarwood, geranium, and mandarin.

Beauty Tip
Make sure to put on sunscreen at least half an hour before you leave the house in order to give your skin time to "drink" it in. When you come home for the day, your first stop should be the washroom to wash off the sunscreen, because it can cause some women to breakout. Even if you're not prone to acne, it's a good idea to wash it off and then moisturize to return your skin back to its normal status quo.

Once thoroughly mixed, apply Avocado Delight to your cheeks, rubbing and moving in an outward circular motion, using a hand on each cheek. Move to the nose; continue rubbing scrub into the skin, then move to the bridge of the nose, exfoliating that area. Move to the forehead and then the chin. Make sure you cover every area of the face. Don't forget your neck. The neck is a part of the face and needs exfoliating to help fight against aging skin. And make sure to avoid getting Avocado Delight in your eyes. You can work around the eye area, but with caution.

Scrub it into the skin for about 3–5 minutes, increasing circulation and blood flow. As a result, oxygen is brought to your cells, which keep cells healthy. Rinse.

The skin is left soft, supple, hydrated and vibrant. All surface dead skin has been removed and the skin is hydrated as a result of the avocado's natural oils.

Avocado is also rich in vitamin B, vitamin E, and vitamin K. Your skin will feel and look more alive, and the pure essential oils have a positive affect on not only your skin, but on your senses as well. That's why it's great to pick your favorite scent!

Whole Foods carries pure essential oils at a good price. Pure essential oils are true plant oils expressed from actual plants. The use of pure essential oils are best because fragrance oils are chemically processed and could cause irritation or symptoms from allergies.

(Thanks to Kimberly King, Licensed Esthetician. Email: bellaking77@yahoo.com)

another pot of green tea facial

We are huge green tea advocates because the stuff is so powerful when it comes to weight loss, and also as an antioxidant. Green tea is a great way to de-puff your skin and to also create the clarity women search for in their complexion. Green tea facials at spas are expensive, and the good news is you can create one at home for pennies. This calming green tea mask should be gently smoothed on your skin. It will make your complexion more even-toned by alleviating blotchiness and more youthful by hydrating the skin.

3–5   **tea bags**
1   **tablespoon plain yogurt**
½   **teaspoon cornstarch**

Brew an extra strong cup of green tea. Stir together one tablespoon of tea with the yogurt and cornstarch. Chill in the fridge for an hour.

Smooth over clean skin and relax for 15 minutes. Splash off with warm water.

ice, ice baby face reviver

It's an old movie star trick used by Bette Davis and Joan Crawford: A kisser full of ice water will close your pores and make you look younger. It's true that splashing your face with cold water (as cold as you can stand it) is an age-old, tried-and-true way to perk up your skin and give it a rosy glow while closing your pores. (The saggier your pores, the more your skin will wrinkle and lines will form). New research indicates that you don't have to go for an ice bath in order to help your skin. If you drink at least four glasses of very cold ice water a day, it will rush the blood flow to every part of your body, including your face, while getting rid of any body bloat. It will also move the toxins out of your system. Each morning and night, throw this idea over the top by splashing the ice cold water on your face to stimulate circulation, de-puff, and even further close those pores. By the way, if you're dragging, or even a little bit tired, there is nothing like that icy water hitting your skin to revive you. Have you ever seen a tired penguin? We didn't think so.

whitening mask

Even though we love a great tan, there's nothing better than flawless skin. If you don't have the skin type that can lend itself to porcelain skin, then it's worth working on having this sort of photo-op perfection.

Here is a whitening secret that will purify, lighten and make your skin glow. This mask is especially helpful in smoothing out a blotchy, uneven complexion. For best results, do this two times a week. This is from Julie Gabriel of *The Green Beauty Guide*.

The secret ingredient is chopped parsley, an aromatic herb full of essential oils. Due to the high content of natural whitening enzymes, parsley is very effective in whitening skin and teeth. The sour cream adds a blend of nourishing proteins and exfoliating lactic acid that will help remove dead skin cells. Add mashed cucumber pulp for even stronger, natural whitening action.

Beauty Tip
After this treatment, try drinking a fresh glass of lemon juice. It's a great way to flush out your system, and a star secret for losing weight. The lemon cleans out toxins from your liver and makes your body a fat-burning machine.

This mask can be stored in a fridge for two days.

3   tablespoons sour cream or thick Greek style yogurt
2   tablespoons finely chopped and minced parsley
3   slices of cucumber (approx. half-an-inch each) mashed
    into a pulp

Whisk all ingredients together in a cup and apply a thick layer. It smells a bit like tsatsiki dip or a really good party dip. Please don't bring taco chips into the bathroom with you because you won't have enough dip for your face.

Leave on for 10–15 minutes and rinse off with tepid water. Pat your face dry and apply sunscreen of your choice.

Don't try this one if you're pregnant. Parsley has estrogenic properties and can even stimulate milk production in women. So if you're pregnant, you need to skip this one because you don't need any more estrogen in your diet. You might also consider skipping parsley in food while you're pregnant. Just a quick tip from your beauty friends.

the martha washington mask

It's time for a beauty moment in history. This one stars the lovely first lady, Martha Washington, who is featured in Janice Cox's book *Natural Beauty for All Seasons*.

The story goes that during the French and Indian War in 1754, George Washington met and fell in love with the pretty Martha Curtis at a dance. Our future first president married Martha, who was a rich widow with children, in 1759. They say the young George noticed Martha's porcelain complexion, which was her trademark. All the women around the first lady tried to figure out Martha's secret, which she later revealed. It turns out that she used a natural mixture to look like a porcelain doll.

Beauty Tip

You know how we love to tell you about the things in the kitchen that you should use to make your skin and body look younger, healthier, and glowing. However, there is one thing that we have to tell you not to use a lot of on your face, and that is your tap water in the kitchen or bathroom. Doctors from across the country agree that tap water strips the skin of its natural barrier oils and moisture that protects against developing wrinkles! Check for sales at your market, and when you're grocery shopping buy the big gallons of pure water for less than a dollar. It won't cost a lot, but the benefits will be priceless.

1	egg, separated
1	teaspoon honey
¼	teaspoon apple cider vinegar

Beat egg white until frothy. Mix together the egg yolk, honey and vinegar. Fold this into the egg white.

Spread the entire mixture over the face and neck. Leave on for 15–20 minutes. Rinse with warm water and pat dry.

Refrigerate any leftovers and discard after a few days.

turmeric of merit

The beautiful women of India have a beauty secret that makes their skin glow. They make homemade skin scrubs with the spice turmeric—a natural skin exfoliant that gets rid of dead cells so your natural bright skin that's lurking underneath has its day (but not a day in the sun!) Try this recipe, but cool it with the turmeric, using only a tiny bit. Using more can actually stain your skin.

1   tiny pinch of turmeric
1   teaspoon of honey

Mix the turmeric and the honey until they're well blended into a thick paste. Work the substance into your skin and then go play with the dog or the kids for 15 minutes. Come back to the sink and wash it away.

The end result will be softer-than-soft skin that glows from within.

arti-choke your face

The artichoke has been used as a medicine by the ancient Greeks, Romans, and Egyptians as a preventative against many illnesses, including the treatment of jaundice and cirrhosis. It has diuretic properties and even contains an active substance called cynarin, which acts as an antioxidant. It's also chock full of vi-

amy's cheat sheet of ingredients and their benefits

Honey	Honey is one of nature's best anti-bacterials. As a facial, it's great for calming acne and breakouts, brightening and energizing skin. The darker the honey, the more the purities.
Sugar	Sugar is a perfect gentle exfoliator that helps balance the PH levels in skin and is also softening.
Green tea	Green tea is an excellent anti-oxidant.
Ginger root	Ginger Root is warming, stimulating, and improves the circulation. It's also anti-microbial and anti-bacterial, grounding and centering.
Oatmeal	Oatmeal is a gentle scrub for sensitive skin and healing.
Mint	Mint is cooling, anti-inflammatory, improves circulation and is very stimulating.
Cucumber	Cucumber is cleansing, healing, cooling and soothes inflammation.

tamin A and potassium. Artichokes even contain a caffeic acid, which can be useful in beauty treatments for the skin.

Due to the diuretic abilities, the rich antioxidants, the vitamin A and potassium, as well as the caffeic acid, the artichoke provides a bevy of beauty enhancements. We found a wonderful artichoke mask for the face and neck that you will love.

1   **fresh artichoke heart, well-cooked, or canned hearts in water (not oil)**
2   **teaspoons of olive oil or canola oil**
½   **teaspoon fresh lemon juice**

Mash the artichoke heart in the oil. Stir in the lemon until you create a paste. Layer the mixture onto the face and neck. Leave this on your face for 15 minutes. Rinse with warm water and then pat dry.

soy what?

Another day, another facial. Please don't say, "Soy what?" We vouch that this one works wonders because the odds are stacked for it. We all know about the health boosts of eating soy or pouring it into our lattes. Now it's time to get a little face time with this healthy drink by giving your kisser a very green soy milk facial.

½   **cup of chilled soy milk (original, and try to avoid the flavored soy milks)**
1   **washcloth**

Measure ½ cup of cold soy milk and place in a bowl. Take a clean washcloth and soak in the soy milk. Ring out the washcloth and then carry it over to your cushiest couch or favorite chair.

Recline, relax, and place the open washcloth over your face. Close your eyes for 15 minutes and let the soy soak in.

Your skin will glow after this treatment because soy is a natural skin brightener. An added benefit is that it contains a form of plant estrogen and will even help reduce or prevent fine lines and wrinkles. This is a once-a-week treatment, but sitting on the couch with a cold compress and your eyes closed is something we prescribe as a daily event.

moving-mountains pimple zapper

There's nothing quite like being over 40 and dealing with hot flashes and zits at the same time. Yes, you can cry the unfair blues, or you can do something about it. By the way, we also feel for all the teenage girls out there who wake up in the morning to see what mountain has erupted overnight. Look, there's Rushmore…and that one on the left is the Grand Canyon. P.S.: We have a secret treatment that really works for all ages—and costs almost nothing. The end result is priceless.

Nasal decongestant

This is an easy one, just take a tiny bit of nasal decongestant and put it on top of your zit. The product is known for getting rid of inflammation and redness, and this includes pimples! The great news is the redness of the pimple is almost immediately gone.

wrong number

You wash. You tone. You moisturize with just the right product. You're over 18. So why does your face occasionally (and more often now than before) break out in unsightly blemishes on your cheeks? The answer might be a serious medical case of cellphoneitis.

To wit: You talk on your cell phone about two hours a day, holding it up to one cheek—the one that seems to break out more. But do you ever clean your phone? Probably not. The end result is bacteria from your skin lingering on your phone plus oil from your skin smearing onto your phone. There's nothing that says *giganto blemish* faster than pressing a little bacteria and oil to one side of your face for a nice hour-long gab session with your girlfriends.

A great idea is to take a paper towel and a little cleaner that's safe for cell phones, or a damp washcloth with a little alcohol on it, and clean the inside of your phone every other day. Or take an acne pad or a cotton ball with a small amount of rubbing alcohol on it and swipe it over your entire phone—cover and inside. Make sure to really clean the keypad because your hands are full of germs, and then you dial. Leave your phone open so it can air dry. The alcohol in either the acne pad or the rubbing alcohol will get rid of the germs. If you use the acne pad, you're better off because it also contains salicylic acid that removes oil and dirt from your cell phone.

butt seriously (for your face)

We don't normally advocate a raid on your precious baby's nursery for beauty purposes, but there are times when a new mom must do what famous bank robbers have always done: *Steal now and think later about getting caught.* Now let's say that you, new mommy, haven't had time for a nice facial (or shower) and your pre-child complexion has gone by the wayside. It's dry with flaking skin and even feels rough to the touch.

Solution: Grab Junior's or other diaper rash cream. Yes, put it right on your own kisser. It works because this product contains zinc oxide and aloe, so your skin with be soothed and healed at the same time for a whooping six dollars. Later, you can always make it up to Junior and buy him or her a car.

potato salad facial without the carbs

From Kym: For years and years in the summer, it seemed that every church picnic featured my Aunt Helen bringing her trademark potato salad. One year when Aunt Helen arrived at the family summer gathering, I took notice that her skin was amazingly smooth, clear and glowing for her sixty years. We had a few moments together near the swings, pushing the little ones, and I just had to ask what she used on her skin. To my surprise, Aunt Helen announced it had to do with her potato salad. Yes, potato salad! She actually calls her secret, "Miracle Whip Miracle for Dry Skin!" (Aunt Helen is very religious.)

The vinegar in the mayonnaise causes the exfoliation and then rejuvenation of the skin cells. The oil in the salad dressing helps to soothe and nourish the skin as it removes the dead flaky skin.

1   tablespoon Miracle Whip

Apply a thin layer from your neck up to below the eyes. The vinegar smell may bother you. In fact, it is strong, so make a fan and breeze the fumes away from your eyes. Leave on for 10 minutes.

Massage the face gently and the dead skin cells will roll off in rubbery little balls. Rinse with warm water. Pat dry.

Do this every day. In six to eight weeks, your skin should be completely renewed.

no-shine complexion treatment

½   cup orange juice
1   tablespoon cornstarch
**   Sprinkle of salt**

It's annoying to wash your face and then about ten minutes later glance in a mirror and gasp at the slight shine that is back. This happens because your cleanser is probably stripping your skin of moisture, which makes your oil glands work extra hard to protect your skin.

You can stop the madness by combining the orange juice, cornstarch and salt in a small bowl. Put this mix on your face and leave it there for 10 minutes.

Rinse with warm water. The citric acid in the juice will clean your face while the cornstarch and salt will remove oil, but won't dry out your skin. This means your oil glands will shrug and say, "We're not needed here." The end result is a beautiful shine-free face for several hours.

apricot facial

1 apricot

If you want a baby smooth complexion and silky, soft skin that doesn't age, then grab an apricot from the fruit bowl on the kitchen table. Apricots fight against premature aging because the fruit has a rich supply of lycopene migrate, which can have a lasting effect on your skin and also works as an antioxidant that rejuvenates skin. This time around you must eat the apricot. By the way, a recent study in Germany indicated that eating apricots would reduce your tiredness by 29 percent.

cornstarch facial

1 tablespoon of cornstarch
½ cup of orange juice
   A sprinkle of salt

If you're a little oily and warm weather only makes your shiny face worse, then try this in a pinch. Facial cleansers strip the skin of moisture, sending your oil glands into overdrive.

Put an end to the vicious cycle by combining: ½ cup of orange juice, 1 tablespoon of cornstarch, and a sprinkle of salt in a bowl.

Smooth over the skin and leave on for 10 minutes. Rinse. The astringent quality of the citric acid in the juice cleanses pores, while the cornstarch and salt combo lift oils without drying out the skin.

SECOND COURSE *hair recipes*

my hair will have what she's having

Far be it from us to neglect any beauty tip from a Victoria's Secret supermodel. So when we heard that beauty Miranda Kerr had an amazing tip for shiny hair to restore her hair—after it was scorched and ironed during Aussie Fashion Week—we listened and felt your pain, Miranda. She insisted that all was not lost, it was not time to power shop in despair, and that this simple recipe restores shine and bounce—and it comes from her pantry.

1   tablespoon of juice from a fresh lemon
1   teaspoon of olive oil

Mix the lemon and olive oil and then liberally slather your hair with it, focusing on putting more of the product on split ends. When you wake up, your dry, straw-like hair will be restored, glossy, and super shiny.

One note: Just make sure you don't do this on the night you invite George Clooney over or on new pillowcases because the residue from the oil will wreck your good linens.

vodka hair

Just when we're already loving vodka for the fact that it has fewer carbs than wine, we heard stunning news from our favorite colorist, Marie Robinson, at the Sally Hershberger Downtown Salon in NYC. Did you know that vodka is a natural way to highlight your hair (and get real relaxed and mellow while you're working on your beauty regime)?

Just combine half a cup of fresh-squeezed lemon juice with three tablespoons of vodka. Get out your favorite spray bottle and give your entire head a spritz, or spritz just pieces that you want to highlight. The booze will swell your hair shaft, which means the lemon can deeply penetrate down to your hair shaft.

The last step is to go out in the sun for two hours, which is the time it takes for the lemon to really kick in. We know that's a lot of UVA, so slather on the sunscreen and bring a good book. Please don't bring the rest of the bottle of vodka sans the three tablespoons you used to look fabulous.

Beauty Tip

This could be filed under hair apparent: If you're bored with your hairstyle and can't really afford a consultation and cut at the fancy salon in town then consider a zero-cost way to have a new look. Switch your part to the other side of your head. You will instantly achieve new hair volume because that hair has a history of going the other way, and it's not about to lie down on the job when it comes to this new change. It will struggle a bit, but you will win thanks to roots that aren't already dented from a constant style. By the way, if you have the Rocky Balboa of tough hair strands then simply go the distance by giving the roots a little squirt of spray to set them. Now smile when everyone asks you if you have a new cut.

sometimes you feel like a coconut, sometimes you don't

1   cup of unsweetened coconut milk

Pour one cup of coconut milk (the unsweetened kind) into a bowl the night before you want to do this treatment. Chill it overnight and wake up to find one solid mass of coconut oil in your fridge.

Proceed to your bathroom and take small handfuls of the solid coconut and work it gently into your dry hair, avoiding the top of your scalp where hair is thinner, but focusing on the ends and working your way up to your ears.

Now, go about your life for the next half hour and then hit the shower or tub and rinse out the concoction. Yes, you will smell like a tropical drink, but the even better news is your hair will be silky smooth for days with no frizzies and sealed ends.

foam your dome

The three givens in life: death, taxes, and shampoo buildup. The latter is that sad day when applying your favorite brand of shampoo is like putting molten lead on your hair. Suddenly, that *wow* shampoo has you looking in the mirror and saying *yow*. Don't be a hater and toss your suds in the garbage. Just do a simple, economical residue treatment to get rid of the excess shampoo build-up that has formed on your locks. An easy trick is to grab your non-foam face wash, one of our favorites is Cetaphil, and wash your hair with it. Why Cetaphil? It's gentle enough that many hospitals use it to wash the hair of babies and small children. It also lacks detergent and won't hurt your hair. Give yourself one rinse if you have only a little bit of build-up and two if your hair feels quite weighed down by life, kids, grocery shopping, and your regularly scheduled shampoo.

my hair needs a bagel with that conditioner

From Cindy: There's nothing like being a natural brunette who has decided to be a "natural" blonde. No, it's not the Chicago sun that's creating that effect, but our chemical friends visiting every six weeks courtesy of a salon that tries to be gentle. But there are days when dry hair that looks tired seems here to stay. Here's a great, quick treatment that adds moisture to over-processed hair.

1	egg
2	tablespoons cream cheese
2	tablespoons butter
2	tablespoons water

Mix all of the above in your food processor or with a whisk. Comb it through your hair with a wide-toothed comb until the mixture is everywhere. Make sure to use any extra on the ends.

Leave on for 15 minutes. Wash in warm water. The end result is silky, healthy-looking processed hair. By the way, hold the lox.

Beauty Tip

If you are having a flat hair day and want a little boost, then just sneak over to your husband's medicine cabinet and steal his shaving cream. Squeeze out a ping-pong ball size of shaving cream and apply it to your damp hair (on the roots) like a mousse. Blow dry. Shaving cream is almost weightless and it's also free of alcohol, so it will give you instant volume and lift. One word of warning: It will dry out your hair if you use it too much, so it's a lift that you should save for a few times a month. Oh, and put the shaving cream back, please. You know how you feel when he doesn't return your moisturizer.

dye job do-over

So you went to get a touch up and your hairdresser was obviously going through a bad break-up, didn't listen to one word you said, and made your hair too dark. Yes, there are always tears and blame, but those won't correct the problem. (Try to be Zen...try again, you can do it!) A better solution is to go home and grab your dishwashing solution off the kitchen sink. Yes, it's Ivory Liquid (or your choice of soap) to the rescue. Add 3–4 drops of the liquid to your bottle of shampoo and shake so it mixes in. Wash you hair using just one shampoo treatment. The dishwashing liquid will lift your color a shade or two. Be careful if you have highlights because it will lift the color off *everything*.

cap it off

Now we finally have a reason to snag those ugly hotel plastic (oh, the horror!) shower caps. You need them for deep conditioning treatments. Slather on the hair conditioner of your choice while in the steamy shower and immediately put on one of those lovely plastic shower caps. The steam from the shower, combined with the plastic, will produce steam inside the cap and make your deep

Beauty Tip

Is your hair a little bit oily these days? The culprit could be what you're eating. If you're suddenly eating a lot of spicy foods with chilies, you could be causing your head to sweat and thus produce more oil. Cut back on curry dishes, which cause a similar sweating problem. If your hair looks extra dry, you could be missing some essential fatty acids in your diet. Try eating more nuts, fish, and seeds. If you have slow hair growth, try Biotin (in pill form), which will help hair accelerate growth while also becoming thicker. You can also find Biotin naturally in foods including eggs, milk, and nuts. Thin hair can get a boost by eating more iron, which can be found in red meat and dark green vegetables.

conditioner work twice as well from the heat. Leave the cap on and take a nice, long, relaxing shower. Yes, shave your gams! You're doing it for your hair! You can remove the cap and rinse before you get out of the shower...or if you're going to hang out around the house, keep the cap on longer for even glossier hair. Later, rinse off the conditioner and pop the plastic cap into your recycle bin.

no fade c

Whether you're a ravishing redhead, bold and beautiful brunette, or bombshell blonde, you don't want your color to fade into the sunset. This is especially true for our *Recessionistas* out there who are hurting when they pluck down $100-plus a month to go gorgeous. We have a great way to make your color hold extra strong for weeks past your usual touchup.

1   packet of a vitamin C supplement powder. (You may have Emergen-C on hand or you can find it at the grocery store) Water

Beauty Tip

Dying for smooth, straight hair like Angelina or Demi? Celebrity hairstylist Peter Butler says that castor oil—yes, castor oil—is a great way to whip up this kind of look-at-me shine. "It's a hairstylist secret, and it's the most fantastic, affordable styling product that will work on any hair type. It actually conditions hair as it styles," he says, noting that he uses it on models with every hair color and type, from Chanel Iman's dark, straight locks, to Marisa Miller's bouncy, blond waves. Butler's oil of choice is the $3.39 Always Natural Castor Oil, and he suggests applying some product to your palms, rubbing your hands together, and then applying the oil to hair by running your fingers through the ends. Finish by running a flatiron over the length and then watch out for blinding shine!

Combine one packet of a vitamin C supplement powder and add enough water to make a thick paste. Shampoo and rinse your hair as usual.

Apply the paste mixture to your wet hair. Leave in for ten minutes and then wash and rinse.

This no-fade formula works because the vitamin C supplement contains high concentrations of ascorbic acid and citric acid, which dissolve the iron and alkaline deposits in hard water that cause color-treated hair to turn dull and mousey. C, we told you we would help make you more beautiful!

tea for your hair

Tea based on your hair color (see below)
Water

It's tough in the recession to keep running to the hair salon for expensive color touch-ups. You don't need to if you simply purchase various teas that can enhance color and add shine to your glorious mane.

All you need to do is choose a tea based on your shade, brew, and then cool to room temperature as a rinse after you shampoo.

You should leave the tea on for 3–10 minutes or from 20–30

Beauty Tip

Between carpool, last-minute homework, and scrambling for something to pack for lunch, there was absolutely no time for you to indulge in a shower this morning, and now your hair is a flattened down mess. If you have five minutes, we have a quick fix: Simply measure out half a teaspoon of baking soda and mix with half a teaspoon of baby powder. Each works wonders in different ways after you shake a little bit into your hair and brush out. The baking soda will take away any product left in your hair while the baby powder is like a sponge for the oil. Flip your head over, give it one big last brush, and voila, instant body without the attached-to-your scalp look.

minutes for a deeper and bolder effect. Choose tea based on your shade:

- Black hair: Golden monkey, Fujian province, wild ginger, Ceylon, Chinese Black tea with ginger.

- Dark Brown: Earl Grey, Ceylon black, or bergamot tea.

- Brown: Summer berry, black tea with elderberry, blackberry, or raspberry.

- Red: Rooibus, Washington state lavender.

- Blonde: Classic chamomile.

warm up your conditioner

We love the idea of walking around for a whole day with conditioner in our hair for a deep treatment, but frankly our bosses wouldn't really appreciate that in the workplace, and our neighbors might think we are very, very strange. And the whole idea of sleeping in hair conditioner is nice, but not exactly the recipe for romance with the mate. Here's a quick kitchen tip on how to make your conditioner sink in deeply in much less time.

Beauty Tip

You've spent a good amount of time in the pool, you unnatural blonde you, and suddenly your hair is looking sadly greenish from the chlorine. Take a deep breath and stay away from the deep end. Here's a great tip from the Bellagio Spa in Las Vegas: Just get out a bottle of ketchup! Red and green are on the opposite ends of the color spectrum. If you take a teaspoon of ketchup and wash your hair with it, the green will be removed by the red coloring of the tomatoes. Finish by shampooing well with your regular favorite, and then condition. It might take a few treatments with the ketchup to work. But don't blame us for any strange burger cravings after you get out of the shower.

Your regular hair conditioner
A microwave-safe bowl

Warm as much conditioner as you like to use in a microwave-safe bowl for 15–20 seconds.

Now, take this warm, but not too hot, treatment and slather it on your hair.

Condition for as long as you have time, knowing that the heat from micro-waving has opened up your hair cuticle, which means that the conditioner is deeply penetrating your entire hair shaft.

Rinse your hair...and that bowl.

getting a lasting high (lights)

The worst thing about great salon highlights is that each time you wash your hair, a little bit of your new vibrant color is fading away. If you like to swim, then maybe your light-colored locks have turned a Shrek-like green, which is horrifying. Before you race back to the salon for another expensive treatment, try this kitchen cure. Take one aspirin and crush it between two spoons. Add to your favorite shampoo and then wash your hair. The salicylic acid in the aspirin will easily take away that horrid chlorine buildup and it will also add shine to highlights that are fading.

Beauty Tip

You can blame it on sleepwalking or sleep carb-loading. You grab that teeny tiny midnight snack and then grab a can of soda to go with it. Stop right now. According to a study in the *Journal of Clinical Practice*, drinking cola at night, or anytime during the day, makes your muscles feel weaker and increases your feelings of exhaustion. The problem is, your soda is loaded with that bad caffeine plus glucose and fructose. Suddenly, your body's potassium takes a dive, and that's the mineral that helps your muscles function properly.

diy disaster: hair

So you tried a home-coloring job and ended up with more dye on your forehead, cheeks, and neck than your actual hair. Many magazines recommend using a dye remover, but that's sim-
ply too harsh for your skin and can cause rashes and irritations. A better way is to hit the bathroom and grab your tube of toothpaste. The key here is it can't be gel, but regular white toothpaste. Take a little bit of it, rub it between your fingers, and then use it over your stained skin to remove the dye. If you have a stubborn stain, then just keep working the toothpaste in until your skin returns to its normal color. Toothpaste contains little microbes that whiten and scrub at the same time, but aren't as harsh on your skin as dye remover.

> ### Beauty Tip
> *You can also mix one tablespoon of mashed avocado with two tablespoons of honey and apply to a clean, washed face. Let it set for ten minutes and then wash. Your skin will have an instant youthful and dewy glow.*

avocado head

Don't hold the guac—at least when it comes to your tresses. One of the most economical ways to have sleek, shiny hair doesn't come out of a bottle, but in your fruit and veggie aisle. Buy a ripe avocado, get rid of the pit, and mash it up in a bowl. All you need to do from here is to dunk your hair in water, towel dry to get rid of excess water, and then smooth the avocado mixture along your tresses. Wait it out for ten minutes, either relaxing in the tub or even throwing in a load of laundry. Go back and make sure you thoroughly rinse out the mix and then you can shampoo and even condition as normal. What you've just treated your hair to is a mixture of avocado rich vitamins, including A, D and E, plus essential fatty-acids and potassium. The vitamin and mineral stew in an avocado works to actually get inside your deepest hair follicles and really give you a deep-conditioning treatment that can't be beat. Your hair will even temporarily retain more moisture for a lasting shine.

sour cream dream

There's nothing like finding a real use for a high-fat product that never really touches your lips anymore. That doesn't mean it can't touch your locks. A few staples that we love with Mexican food—avocados, sour cream, and lemon juice— are also great for your hair. Please don't eat a bag of taco chips while doing this treatment, but if you must, please pass them over to us.

1   **ripe avocado**
2   **tablespoons sour cream**
    Juice of half a lemon
1   **towel**

Beauty Tip

We love this little celebrity insider trick that focuses on how the young A-list starlets have that sexy, tousled, unkempt, but still perfect hair. Just grab your bathroom soap bar. Celebrity stylist, Sally Hershberger, says to just take a bar of soap in your hands with a little water. Work your fingers through your damp hair before blow-drying. Sally says this also reduces static and flyaway strands. Her favorite pick is Ivory soap, which costs two dollars at drugstores.

Cut the avocado in half, take out the pit. Scoop out the fleshy meat, and mash until it's smooth. Add the sour cream and the juice of half a lemon. Stir well.

Take this gorgeous, high-caloric gunk and run it through your hair and on top of your strands. Don't be afraid to really work it deep into your scalp while giving yourself one of those nice little relaxing massages.

Take a warm towel that's fresh out of the dryer or a hotel shower cap that you've "borrowed" and cover your hair with it.

Wait 20 minutes, jump in the shower, and make sure to shampoo and not just rinse. Olé! You now have hair that's so soft to the touch you won't be able to stop feeling it either.

P.S.: Make sure that gunked-up towel immediately hits the laundry room after you give it an initial rinsing to de-goop it. There's nothing like your husband grabbing for your avocado towel by mistake and wiping sour cream and avocado all over his freshly showered body!

Flat head

There's nothing quite like hair that naturally wants to collapse against your scalp like it has given up its will to live. Here's a quick recipe for revival.

Beauty Tip

In a rush and no time for a shower? Throw your hair up in a neat pony-tail, but let your probably greasy, flat bangs fall on your forehead. Carefully, grab a dab of shampoo, and in the bathroom sink just wash your bangs. You can even give a spritz of leave-in conditioner. Blow dry for three minutes and you look like that shower happened even if it was just a quick sink job.

2   packets of real sugar (please, no sugar substitutes)
1   20-ounce spritzer bottle filled with water

Mix the sugar into a bottle of water. If you can, use bottled water so it's free of chemicals.

Give it a nice shake and then lightly mist your hair with the sweet juice. The sugar will immediately wake up your hair by making the follicles swell a bit without frizzing.

DO-IT-YOURSELF BEVERLY HILLS HAIR COLOR

In this economy, going to a hair colorist every six weeks might seem like another mortgage payment. In Beverly Hills, it's certainly a scene…from Rachel Zoe to Michelle Pfeiffer, along with other various stars plus wives and girlfriends (not necessarily in that order) of the rich and infamous. Everyone is maneuvering for time with the wizards of hair. Everyone has to valet their car, wait for hours for an actual stylists and then be prodded by five, count them, five assistants and assistants to assistants. Finally, you're seated in the chair only to fork over hundreds of dollars for a color that basically looks bright and shiny for a week. Then you're back to the drawing board, waiting for your next fix with the hair genius. No more! Here are a few ways to save a few hard earned Benjamins and keep your color looking fabulous:

for a color enhancer:

Boil one quart of water. In a piece of doubled cheesecloth, add the following:

- For brunettes: a handful fresh rosemary sprigs (crumple in your hand)

- For blondes: a handful of dried chamomile

- For "orange tone" redheads: a chopped-up carrot

- For "berry tone" redheads: a chopped up beet

Tie up the ingredient in the cheesecloth and toss into the boiling water. After a few minutes, remove pot from the heat. Let steep for 10 minutes. Remove and discard the cheesecloth bag. Shampoo and rinse your hair as usual. Then, pour the warm (not hot) color-enhancing rinse over your hair. As a final rinse, use a quart of cold water. Once-a-month treatments will keep your hair color vibrant.

tomato head

There is nothing worse than product buildup, and the way it makes your hair appear so dull. Part of the problem is that your PH balance is also kaflooey. Here's a way to restore your PH and add life and shine to your hair.

1   cup tomato juice
1   teaspoon cornstarch

Mix the cornstarch and the juice. Pour on the top of clean, wet hair.

Wrap your head with an old towel (the juice will stain) and leave on for 10 minutes.

Rinse well. Shampoo again to make sure you're not feeling like a can of Campbell's tomato soup.

Your hair's PH is now restored and you will see incredible shine and body.

brew for you

Beer has always been a natural treatment for dull hair. Hey, our moms were right about this one. The only problem is you might have to pry those two tablespoons out of your husband's hand.

2   **tablespoons beer**
1   **squirt of regular shampoo**

Add the beer to your regular shampoo. Suds up and rinse out.
Your hair will look shiny and have great bounce.

le bubbly hair secret

You must love the French because they know how to combine the finer things in life with beauty. There's nothing like using a little bit of leftover champagne as a beauty treatment as
they do in the City of Love.

½   **cup champagne**
½   **cup hot water**

Shampoo your hair as usual and rinse out the suds. When you're
done, pour the champagne-water over your head. You don't have
to rinse it out. You will see an incredible shine if you leave the mixture on your hair and rinse it out next time you're in the shower.

hair raisers

BCB Tip: If you want a salon quality blow-out at home instead of the $50-plus tip to your stylist then follow these simple
rules:

- Buy a cheap microfiber towel for $10 from a
  discount store. A few pats on your hair will remove over 50 percent of the water and cut your
  drying time in half.

- Blot the water and then divide your hair into one- or two-inch sections. Pin the rest of your hair to the top of your crown with clips. The rule is, the smaller the section of hair you're drying, the smoother and straighter it will blow out.

- With your jumbo brush, wrap your hair and dry, moving your dryer from the highest point (think Minnesota on a map) to the lowest while gently pulling your hair down towards Texas.

- Keep going until all the pins are out. Don't brush out your finished "pieces" until a few minutes after you're done with the blowout. Let the hair settle down and then it won't frizz.

oh baby

If you can't get rid of annoying flyaway hair then rush into your nursery and borrow a little bit of baby lotion. It's a great hair hydrator that breaks the static electricity that made your hair a flyaway mess in the first place. An added bonus is that it's so thin it won't gunk up your hair or cause it to stick to your scalp. The best treatment is to take a dime size of baby lotion, rub it into your hands, and then go over the flyaways very gently. Or, you can put your hair into a ponytail holder, run your hands down the ponytail just once—twice is too much—and then when you release the ponytail, your hair will be silky smooth. Oh and thank little Junior for "borrowing" her products.

to-dye-for trick

1   Chapstick

You're about to color your hair at home to save money, and we applaud you. But stop right there and put the dye down right now! Now, please rush to your purse and find your Chapstick. This might sound crazy, but you will thank us later. Rub the Chapstick on your skin by your hairline and don't be stingy with it. You're creating a barrier around your face, so the dye doesn't color your face. This works because wax doesn't mix with dye... and wax wins every time when it comes to making the dye retreat. Later your mate might say, "Honey, your hair looks beautiful, but what is that cherry smell on your face?" You don't have to dye and tell.

java for your hair

There's nothing wrong with adding a little more java to your life. This time around you won't get the jitters because this coffee is for your hair. One word of warning: This is not for blondes. You can try it if your hair is red, black, or brown.

5   cups warm coffee that has been brewed

Shampoo as usual and then condition. When you're done, pour the coffee on top of your hair. This is a leave-in treatment that will make your hair color appear deeper and create amazing shine.

scarf treatment

This is a quick European beauty trick that some of the world's biggest beauties have done for years. Wash and dry your hair as usual. When you're done, find a clean silk scarf. Rub it over your entire head of hair. Do this with a light touch, but only once. The end result will be hair that has more body and shines like crazy.

french-know-best cleanser

It's all about multi-tasking when it comes to living life and using products! Do you have a headache, need to just clear your head, or want a good scalp cleansing as a side effect? This French formula will do it *all* in one clean sweep. It's from a wonderful aromatherapist, author, and natural health expert, Julia Meadows.

1   rose with petals removed
1   oz. apple cider vinegar
1   oz. aloe vera gel
1   oz. Witch Hazel extract
1   oz. unflavored vodka
     Enough distilled or spring
     water to cover petals

Beauty Tip

Here's an eye-opening tip. Let's say you're putting on makeup and notice that your mascara is either missing or it's dryer than a desert. Try a favorite natural trick of makeup artists. Take out your lip balm, coat one finger lightly, and then add a touch of black eyeliner to your finger. Simply put this on an old mascara wand and coat your lashes, or put it on with your fingertips for a little bit of definition. By the way, this is a great way to condition your eyelashes.

Place the rose petals in a glass jar and pour the liquid ingredients over them to cover Leave to steep for several hours. Strain the liquid and discard the rose petals. Apply to hair generously. Rinse and enjoy your newly beautiful hair!

sweet-and-sticky shine

From Kym: When I was a young reporter working the beat in the Upper Peninsula of Michigan, it was a beautiful country, but very, very cold. I remember being sent out to do a story on tapping trees to get the pure, wholesome maple syrup. After one taste of the pure stuff, I could never turn to Aunt Jemima again.

It was in the wild woods of the UP, as it is fondly called, that I noticed that so many of the women who spent most of their time in the outdoors had wonderfully shiny and soft hair. Mine was getting dryer and more brittle by the minute from being out in the extreme below-zero temperatures covering news stories all day. Finally, I asked a few of the more outdoorsy women what there hair secret was. They revealed that it was not from a bottle, but from a tree. What I needed was sap.

As beauty writer, Janice Cox, says, "Maple sap is a colorless watery solution that contains sugar, various acids, and salts. That is why pure maple syrup is a treat for dry, damaged hair. It restores lost moisture and gives hair extra body and shine." And it's great on your morning breakfast hot cakes.

½   **cup of pure maple syrup**

Pour the syrup onto clean, dry hair and massage into the scalp and ends.

Wrap hair in plastic shower cap or Saran Wrap. Leave on hair for 20–30 minutes. Rinse well with warm water.

gel-oh

It's another one of those mornings where you look in the mirror and see that your eyes look bigger (nice), your nose is larger (oh, no) and your chin seems even more pronounced (the horror). Blame your hair, because it's just so flat—thanks to cold weather or buildup of product—that it looks like you have a swimming cap permanently attached to your scalp. Of course, the answer is to wash and blow dry, but that's not a real solution because your flat hair is now just flat, clean hair. Stop and put your curling iron down, right now. We can see you—take that hair spray can out of your hands and grab some shaving gel. Yes, shaving *gel*, but not shaving *cream*.

Squeeze out a nickel-sized plop of gel and work it through your now-dry hair, beginning at your crown and moving down. Keep scrunching small portions of gel throughout your entire mane. Now, shake out your head of hair. It's amazing that your hair has virtually doubled in size on a fullness level. The gel has a way of making your hair shaft swell a bit, which makes your leg hair easier to shave. That same little power "booster" also cures your flat head. Now, stop staring at your hair and do remember to shave those gams.

Beauty Tip

Top hairstyling pros tell their clients to invest in a cheap tube of clear mascara. Next time your hair decides to have a frizzy day, just run a little clear mascara between your thumb, first, and middle finger. Now, apply it to the frizz. Your new straight hair will last all day long.

gone bananas

We scoured the globe to find beauty tips and tricks for you, and we noticed that the women of the tropics seem to have one thing in common besides gorgeous bodies and wonderful tans. They all have shining, soft, glowing hair. The how is partly because they're big fans of bananas. So your beauty spies visited a few hair salons on the islands and noticed that the locals all used this lovely yellow fruit in their hair concoctions.

Bananas and honey make an excellent combination and conditioner for your hair because they are rich in potassium and vitamins A, B, and C. This combo coats the hair cuticle, while adding moisture and shine, and the hair feels and looks thicker.

1   **banana**
1   **tablespoon honey**

Mix together the banana and honey. Wet the hair and pour the mixture on your scalp. Wrap your hair in a plastic shower cap and leave on for 20 minutes. Rinse well, shampoo, and condition as usual.

got grease?

Your alarm clock didn't go off and there is absolutely no time to deal with your hair. The problem is, you didn't deal with it last night after you worked out, and now it's a greasy mess. Grab your big flat paddle brush and lightly mist it with hair spray. Brush your hair one time—and only once. The grease will attach to the sticky spray. Now, on a cool setting, lightly blow-dry your hair, and it will fluff back into your regular, no-grease style.

shine on

Why is it that some women not only have great hairstyles, but their hair also has the perfect shine that always catches the light? Don't hate them because they're dutiful about their shine routines. Just try this simple recipe that they are probably doing at home.

2   tablespoons, apple-cider vinegar
1   pinch of baking soda
1   small squirt of shampoo

In a small bowl or paper cup, mix the above ingredients and use as a once a week shampoo. The vinegar will strip your hair of product buildup while the baking soda will neutralize any acids that have built up.

Condition as normal and your hair should shine on for days.

pool cue

You love to swim. It has slimmed your hips and made your legs look amazing, but your hair is one big brassy mess. The cure involves one of our favorite home treatments: aspirin. Just crush an aspirin tablet and put it in your bottle of shampoo. Wash and rinse. The acid in the aspirin will work on getting rid of the chlorine that's stuck in your hair (and making it brassy). It will only take one or two washes and you'll be back to your regular gorgeous color.

mane event

3   **bags of black tea**
2   **cups hot water**

If you're a brunette who worries about her locks fading into some dull washed-out brown color during the hot-weather months, you don't have to pay for expensive hair coloring at the local salon. Just walk into your private kitchen salon, open the cabinet door, and grab a box of black tea.

Steep three bags of black tea in two cups of hot water. Let the mixture cool and then pour it over your hair. Let this sit on your hair for ten minutes and then rinse.

This is a natural way to darken your hair without an expensive, drying treatment that could cost upwards of $100.

THIRD COURSE

mani, pedi, and more recipes

is that a grapefruit on your elbow?

1   grapefruit

If you have rough elbows, then cut a grapefruit into equal halves. Put a towel down on a table and rest one elbow into each half of the grapefruit. The citric acid in the fruit will exfoliate your elbows after a five-minute "dip" into the fruit. When you're done, rub a little extra virgin olive oil on those elbows or apply your favorite moisturizer. This treatment also works great on rough feet.

lifetime ban on dishpan hands

We've all been there...no glam, no glitter, just gunk. You made a big pan of lasagna for dinner and now everyone in the family has entered the "Doing the Dishes Witness Protection Program" and you're left with your hands in icky dishwater for the next 20 minutes. Let your beauty guides here remind you that nothing is as drying as harsh dishwater soap.

One great solution (for pennies) is to grab your box of baking soda from the fridge. Now, fill the sink with warm water and that drying soap offender, but also add a healthy tablespoon of baking soda to the water and give the sink a quick stir with your hands. The baking soda will neutralize the acids in the water and leave your skin feeling like silk. One added benefit is it will also make your sink cleaner and looking brand-new. Now, if you could only find someone to wash those dessert dishes.

mon cinnamon body scrub

Oh, there is nothing like a little cinnamon in your coffeecake or even iced tea—one of Cindy's favorites with green tea to kill the taste of the tea and level out your blood sugar. Try it. It's delicious! The spice is a great way to keep your blood sugar levels in check, so use it liberally in yogurt and on oatmeal. At Beauty Cookbook Headquarters, we also found a way to take a little bit of this tangy substance and use it as a body scrub that's so delicious you might be tempted to pour the entire thing over ice cream. Please, you don't need the calories, and your skin is begging you to give it this one small pleasure.

1   **cup brown sugar**
1½   **teaspoon cinnamon**
1   **cup of extra virgin olive oil**
1   **plastic bottle**

Beauty Tip

Say something nice to yourself right now. In fact, when you pass a mirror, always try to force yourself to say or think something positive. You don't have to say that you're gorgeous. Just say, "I got a lot done today and I'm proud of myself." Or, try to say, "I just had a great time with my kids and these are memories that will last forever." Just thinking about your good qualities will help you feel better, lower your heart rate, and even make you look prettier to the outside world.

In a small mixing bowl, combine the brown sugar and cinnamon. Please stop thinking about making chocolate chip cookies at this moment. Yes, we can read your mind, so put down the chips. Yes, put them down! Now, you've combined your sugar and cinnamon, so it's time to drizzle the oil into the mixture and use your favorite whisk to blend the ingredients together.

Note: Whisk about five times; you don't want it to be too liquidy.

Pour the mixture into a jar or plastic bottle and proceed directly to the bathroom. You can use this scrub in the shower as a way to get rid of dead skin. The sugar is a natural scrub, and having oil as a back-up is an instant moisturizer. The cinnamon is the secret ingredient because it actually will help bring the blood to the skin's surface and give you a healthy, just-exercised type of glow.

You can keep this mix in your fridge for a week, but then discard and mix up a new bath for just pennies.

Beauty Tip

Make sure after your bath to slather your skin with extra virgin organic coconut oil, which you can find at any organic or natural grocery store. The oil will melt on your skin and make it baby smooth.

detox bath

1   bathtub
1   box of Epsom salt (which you can keep in the bathroom for future detox baths)
     Warm water

Fill your bathtub with warm water and add half a cup of Epsom salt in the bath. Epsom salts will not only detox your entire body, but will revive muscles that might have had a tough day on the job or at the gym. This treatment is especially effective if you have a big event coming up because the salts will also de-puff your skin and make you appear visibly thinner.

fizzy bath (to relieve aching muscles)

4   antacid tablets
Water

Run a warm bath and toss in the four tablets. Soak for 20 minutes in this mixture when your muscles are overextended or swollen. The treatment will reduce swelling and improve blood flow. This works because antacids contain sodium bicarbonate, which gets the blood circulating again, and aspirin to alleviate the pain.

scrub-a-dub

⅓   cup turbinado sugar
2   teaspoons olive oil
½   cup course ground coffee

Mix the sugar with the olive oil and the ground coffee. Stir the mixture lightly and don't liquefy the grounds.

Use this as a full-body scrub that will soften and cleanse your pores.

you've got legs and know how not to abuse them

Gams. Stems. Limbs. All of the above are words for legs, and there is nothing better than having a great pair to show off in skirts or short-shorts. Many times, beauty comes from within, so this is a recipe that will require you to actually eat the following suggestions. Since we're talking about basil here, nothing is quite as good as a fresh mozzarella-tomato-basil salad. Bet you never knew that you aren't just giving your taste buds a treat here; you are also were helping your legs stay beautiful.

2   tablespoons of fresh basil (use in any food you like, such as salad, soup or even on baked chicken or on fish)

All you need to do here is to consume two tablespoons of basil as many days a week as possible. Each time you eat this herb you are ingesting 60 percent of your daily recommended allowance of vitamin K. Stick with us here: The vitamin K helps your body produce a protein called thrombin that helps bring blood to your veins by rerouting the blood away from damaged veins to healthy ones. The end result is a reduction in spider or varicose veins. And the ones that you already are stuck with will fade away with the help of basil. An additional benefit is that you will improve your wrinkles by 66 percent in ten days or less, insist scientists at Kasturba Medical College in India. Basil contains major flavonoids and helps your body synthesize all that youth-appearing, skin-plump collagen that everyone covets. Basil, rich in vitamin A, also helps your skin cells repair and replace themselves, leaving you looking more youthful than ever.

razor-burn rescue

½   cup of aloe vera juice

If your man has burned himself while shaving, or you did a number to your legs while shaving, it's time to hit the bottle…of aloe vera juice.

Pour the juice on a soft washcloth and gently rub the burned area. The natural healing properties of aloe vera will reduce redness, calm irritations, and even reduce some rashes.

don't drag your feet—bag them foot treatment

Oh, those gorgeous heels looked so lovely in the store. You could even take a few steps out of your house without feeling the pain. After a few hours of hobbling around, you have this to say about those wonderful skyscraper shoes: &^%$#! Yes, you have vowed to throw those shoes out the minute you get home and live in flip-flops for the rest of your life. We caution: You cannot wear flip-flops with a nice dress, so please learn how to pamper your poor feet, which gave their all in the name of fashion.

5   **aspirin**
2   **spoons for crushing**
1   **tablespoon of lemon juice**
2   **large plastic bags (such as your grocery store bags)**

Crush five aspirin by placing them between two spoons and turning them into powder. Place the aspirin in a bowl. Mix in the lemon juice until you have a thick paste.

Apply the mixture to your calloused feet and then place a plastic bag around each foot. Please don't tie the bag shut at your ankles because we don't want you cutting off your circulation. It's enough to just put your feet in the bags and with your hand smoosh the bag closed by your ankles.

Sit down and rest for 15 minutes. When you're done, and with the bags still on (so you don't mess up your clean floor), hit the bathroom or sink and wash your feet with warm water.

You will find that the acidic lemon, combined with the acid in aspirin, will remove the dead skin on your feet and leave them silky smooth. This is a great time to use a little bit of moisturizer on both feet to protect the new skin underneath. Suddenly, those heels don't seem so bad.

pineapple pedi (and mani)

Maybe it's all the stress in the air, but you've become someone who—let's confess right here—picks at her nails. Bad, bad, bad. Stop right now! It's heinous enough that you start this deed by picking off old polish, but you also go for your cuticles and then hangnails. Now your hands look like even the most expensive mani wouldn't fix the problem. Well, we have the cure, although your career as a picker should be retired, pretty please. Your cuticles are saying prayers.

1   slice of fresh pineapple
1   damp washcloth

Remove all of your old polish with remover. Now, wash your hands, dry them, and rub that slice of pineapple over your nails and your cuticles. When you're done coating each nail stop and allow the juice to work its way in for 1–2 minutes.

Don't wash your hands again, but simply wipe away the excess juice. The pineapple contains a very powerful enzyme called bromelain that takes off the dead cuticle particles while cleaning and brightening your actual nail.

When you're done with your treatment, find a washcloth and make it a bit damp. Use it to push your cuticles back. They should be looking manicure-ready now.

Note: You can also do this as a pedicure for terrific tootsies.

no-gripes-with-grapes nail treatment

We hate to pick (again), although we know that there are many pickers out there. Yes, we can see you, picking at your poor cuticles when you're worried about the economy or who will win *Dancing with the Stars*. All of a sudden, you look down and your hands look like some sort of ugly zone with ragged, horrible, half-torn cuticles staring up at you in some sort of sad surrender. Try this recipe and give your poor cuticles a little TLC.

5   **grapes**
1   **tablespoon of sugar**
1   **paper plate**

Start by taking a sharp knife and slicing the grapes in half. Next, dip the flesh part of the grape into the sugar, which you've dusted onto a paper plate.

Take your half grape (now crusty from the sugar) and use one to work each cuticle. (You have ten half grapes and will use one for each finger). Your goal is to rub the grape on the ragged parts for about half a minute. Have a warm, damp washcloth on hand to wipe each finger after you're done, so you don't get ultra sticky.

Beauty Tip

If you're having home-pedicure night, grab a large, low plastic pan and fill it with water (leave room at the top, so it doesn't spill when you put your feet in), a little bit of bubble bath, and 12–15 marbles of all shapes and sizes. Start your pedicure with a little home reflexology treatment. Simply dunk your tootsies in the sudsy, sweet- smelling water and run the bottom of your feet along those marbles. It feels great, and even helps to rid your body of toxins. When you're done with this treatment, move on to the grape-cuticle cure and finish with a light coat of polish. You just saved yourself a $50 pedicure, plus had a wonderful, fun evening with the girls.

This works because those grapes contain malic acid, which is actually a mild alpha hydroxy acid. It will get rid of dead skin cells and even loosen up the toughest dead skin. Enter the sugar, which acts as a mild exfoliant and further "sweeps away" the dead skins.

Now, take a nail trimmer and carefully remove any hangnails and trim any stubborn cuticles. This is also a great home pedicure treatment that you can try on yourself, your kids (during an all-girl slumber party), or even your girlfriends.

you've got soles

Need a simple way to get rid of that icky yellow skin on the bottom of your feet? Just run to the fridge and grab a tomato. Cut about half an inch off the top. Rub that part of the tomato over the yellow part of your feet and over any calluses. The acid in the tomato will remove the yellow, while making your feet baby soft. It might take 3–4 treatments before you get back to your original foot color.

clorox me

1   **tablespoon of Clorox**
1   **cup of water**

Beauty Tip

For those of you who bruise easily, eating pineapple is a great way to get rid of dark spots because the bromelain helps them go away faster.

We loved all those dark, vamp nail polish colors that were "in" five minutes ago, but the bad news is that they left your nails an ugly dark yellow because dark polish tends to stain. It's easy to go back to your regular nail color by taking a tablespoon of Clorox and diluting it in a cup of water. Rinse your nails with it and then buff them. The yellow will be gone.

lemon hand

Manis are a girl's best friend, but all that dark polish can really stain your poor nails. We have another very juicy way to fix your polish problem.

1   **fresh lemon**
1   **sharp knife**

Cut the lemon into halves. Remove the dark polish from your nails and wash and dry your hands. Now stick your fingertips into half a lemon— your right hand in one, your left in the other.

Keep that lemon attached to your hands for five to ten minutes. By the time you're done, you will be back to fresh white-ish nails.

Beauty Tip

What about the old tale that you should brush your hair 100 times a day? Stop right now. This actually harms your hair, and might cause you to rip it out while damaging the roots. You just need to brush your hair into a style and then stop and put that brush down. Step away from the hair tools. You're done for the day.

lemon-aide

If you're working around the kitchen with your hands in and out of sudsy water and cold chickens, then the first thing that will dry out from the constant washing or harsh dishwater soap will be your hands. Here's a quick remedy for brittle nails and hands that look tired and old.

6   **tablespoons extra virgin olive oil**
2   **tablespoons lemon juice**

Squeeze a fresh lemon and leave the juice in bowl. Add the olive oil. Take a few minutes and place your entire hand into the bowl.

Leave ample time for the other hand. You can also soak your hands and then put on thin plastic gloves for a deeper conditioning treatment.

Leave on for at least 10–15 minutes. Repeat this treatment nightly. Your nails will stop breaking and your skin will look years younger.

burn, baby, burn

Puffy eyes make us want to cry. Why? Those bags make you feel less attractive and look exhausted. They can even be painful. The culprit here causing the puff is water retention from salty foods you ate last night. (Puffy eyes can also be caused by various health issues, so if this is a problem, check with your doc.)

One universal way we found to get rid of the swollen sad look is to invest in some simple burn pads. These little babies may not be in your kitchen but they could be in your pantry or medicine cabinet. New York City dermatologist, Francesca Fusco, suggests using 2nd Skin Moist Burn Pads, which contain a unique cooling gel made up of 97 percent water. Chill them in your fridge and apply under the eye area for five to ten minutes in the morning. The coolness of the pads constricts blood vessels and reduces swelling, explains Fusco. Plus the individual packets are great for traveling and are also perfect for jet-lagged eyes.

condition your entire body

It never fails. You reach for that bottle or jar of wonderful moisturizer and your husband decides to throw himself a little head-to-toe slathering party. Men can never use just a little dot of cream, but actually feel that they need the entire bottle in order to moisturize one kneecap. You're left with bupkis…and crunchy skin. A quick solution is to jump in the shower, hold the swears, and rinse your body with water. Now, take your favorite hair moisturizer and lather it on your entire body, avoiding your privates—thank you very much! Keep the conditioner on your body and step away from the water. Turn the water on hot and steam up the shower (but don't get burned). Just take in that nice wonderful steam for a few minutes while you actually deep condition your entire body. Rinse with lukewarm water until the product is gone, and then step out of the shower and tell your husband to keep his paws off your beauty products.

Beauty Tip

Did you know that you could beat bloating with chocolate? It's not a joke — nor is it too good to be true. Let's say it's that time of the month and you're craving sweets, feeling moody, and looking like you're six months preggers (and you're just carrying the bulk of extra carbs plus water). Studies show that having a few daily bits of dark chocolate the week before and during your period will help reduce bloating. The flavonoids in the chocolate help you metabolize carbs fast, thus reducing bloating.

red lipstick be gone

We love the new red lipstick look, but we don't like how, even when you wash up, your lips are still the color of fire. Don't run back to your never-problematic nudes; try this trick to return your slightly stained lips back to their natural color.

1   **cotton ball**
    Waterproof eye makeup remover or petroleum jelly

Use a cotton ball soaked with waterproof eye makeup remover to get rid of any pigment. In a pinch you can swipe on a little petroleum jelly to remove the tomato look from your face.

we do mean to brush you off

1   **store-bought body brush. (Do not use your hairbrush, as it is probably too rough on your skin.)**

Chinese women and Hollywood ladies know how to give a great brush off. We don't mean they're rude; they know the benefits of investing in an under-$10 body brush (even found at the supermarket) and using it every single day to keep the cellulite away, while reviving the skin on your body. You will take it all off clothing-wise, and brush your body while you're dry and before you step into the shower. Expect to see little flakes of dead skin fall off of you. A total body brushing (also fun to do with a mate) is a great way to rev up circulation, exfoliate dead skin, and even break up cellulite before it forms. It will also double as an expensive spa treatment, as the brush stimulates your lymphatic system and helps you purge the toxins that rob you of energy and make you look much older.   Simply invest in a natural brush that feels soft to the touch.

You will brush daily for two minutes, starting at your toes and working up to the top of your head. Then it's off to the shower, or a nice warm bath. It's also a boost to brush on the bottom of your feet, behind your knees, and on your neck as a way to work the special areas near your lymph glands.

lip shtick

If you have dry and chapped lips from the winter, a dry climate, or the fact that you're stressed out, you don't have to stress further by buying expensive gels and ointments. Instead, invest in shea butter, sunflower oil, or even beeswax. These are natural ways to keep your lips softer than soft, and these treatments even smooth out lines that develop with age on your lips. So give your pucker some penny-wise help. *Bonus*: Make sure to put these treatments on wet lips (from water, not kissing!). You will seal in the water this way and give your lips an extra moisture booster shot.

hand it to you

Your hands do double and triple duty all day long. When is the last time you did something nice for them? The following is a way to take aging hands and give them a big pick-me-up before they have to pick up things again.

2   **teaspoons sugar**
1   **tablespoon honey**

In a small bowl, mix the sugar and honey. Now use this mixture over your hands and nails to remove any dead skin cells.

Make sure to moisturize when you're done. If you have the time use plastic gloves over your moisturizer to give your hands a deep penetrating treatment. Your can even sleep in the gloves if you want to really give your hands a trip to the Bahamas.

Beauty Tip

You're busy primping for a big night out with your honey. Naturally, you put on your favorite lip-gloss, but it's getting a bit old and thick. You don't have to toss it. Just put on a thin coat of the too-thick mix and then rub an ice cube over your lips. It will restore the shine and cut the glop in half.

breath so sweet

Once upon a time there was a beautiful woman who had lovely hair, wore the right clothes, carried the "It" bag, and had perfect make-up, but she never got a date, and people stood steps away from her on escalators and in long lines because...shhhh... she had breath from hell. Out of mouthwash like our friend? Try this quick recipe to kill all that makes your breath not-so-sweet.

2   tablespoons of lemon juice

Gargle the lemon juice. The citric acid will knock out the bacteria in your mouth that is causing the offensive odor.

rx for cramps

It's that time of the month—and we don't mean when the sales are on at the mall. It's that time when the mind-numbing cramps begin and you start to think, "Maybe it would have been good to have been born...a boy." We've cooked up a little trick for you to get rid of bloat and cramps. Just take some fresh parsley and add it to your foods during the few days before your period. It's great in salads and turkey sandwiches, or even in a fresh stew or crock-pot dish. The herb is nature's diuretic, and it stops salt from entering your tissues. The parsley is also filled with apiol, an estrogen compound that helps cure cramps. It gets rid of a good portion of the water in your system, which might mean you do something completely reckless during that time of the month: Yes, haul out your skinny jeans! Is that even legal?

ingrown groan

Are ingrown hairs a major beauty 911 in your life? An easy fix is on the way.

1   cotton ball
Glycolic or salicyllic-acid toners

Soak the cotton balls in the toners and then wipe them onto your problem areas, avoiding your private parts, of course. In a day or two the hair should pop through the skin—the acid will help break down the dead skill cells covering it.

we can smell you treatment

We realize that if you are reading this beauty book, you almost certainly do not have body odor. You are a natural beauty armed with a battalion of your own secrets and stay-gorgeous tricks at your fingertips. But what's up your sleeves—way, way up? We know your armpits are there and perhaps they are stuck with an extremely hot, muggy, and humid day. There are times when even the best deodorant is no match for Mother Nature. The ladies in Texas are nodding right now.

Note from Cindy: I just did a story for the *Sun Times* where I had to travel to Texas, and between the hair frizz and humidity, the only beautiful thing about me was my nail polish. Wait, that chipped from the heat, too. Okay, there was nothing that screamed "pretty."

What do you do when body odor is a real concern? We have a few perfect tricks. Start with the idea of putting on your regular deodorant before you go to bed the night before a hot day. Your own natural body heat will make the product really sink in and you won't have to reapply in the morning even if you take a shower.

You can also get to know a few BO specifics. For instance, actual sweat has no smell. According to holistic physician Jeffery Morrison, the odor actually comes from bacteria on your skin. We have another great natural solution to absorb and even eliminate the odor-causing bacteria before it can start percolating on your skin. You just need to invest in a bottle of apple cider vinegar.

Experts feel that this actually works better than deodorant because the all-natural cure lowers your skin's PH level, which kills odor-causing bacteria. Try this simple recipe from Dr. Morrison:

1   cotton ball
2   tablespoons apple cider vinegar

Soak a cotton ball in vinegar and apply to your underarms daily. The vinegar smell will dissipate, leaving you smelling as sweet as a peach all day.

lashing out

Not that we want to throw blame at any one star (Brooke Shields), but you really got us thinking that thick, long eyelashes are a must-have accessory. The only problem is we're a bit chicken to get a prescription that costs big bucks and has more warnings on it than we can squint to read. Wait, we could mess up our eye pressure and cause discoloration of our eye color? There are times when the cost of beauty is way too high. But, we still want those lashes without shelling out too much cash or worrying about discolored lids. We talked to a few eyelash extension specialists to find natural secrets to longer and fuller lashes.

One of our favorites, Hannah, of the Michael Joseph Fury salon in California, gave us an old family secret that her Russian grandmother did all the time to her own amazing lashes. Two words: castor oil.

½   teaspoon of pure castor oil

Measure out this small amount of pure castor oil. Dab on your fingers. Apply gently to your lashes and eyebrows, especially the ones that have scanty growth.

Rubbing the oil on each evening will make them grow thick and long.

Beauty Tip
Go to the drugstore and buy the cheapest blue-liner pencil you can find on the shelves. By using the blue liner on your upper and lower lids you will reduce the redness in your tired eyes.

milk-it milk bath

Oops, you did it again. You sat in the sun for a few hours too long because the kids were having a great time on the beach, and now you look like a cross between a burn victim and a red Maine lobster. It's time to go to an old-fashioned, never-fail method that even your grandmother would endorse. Simply go home, get out a bowl and do the following:

1   cup of whole milk (not skim…you need the fat here)
1   cup of ice cubes

Place the ice cubes in a bowl and then pour the whole milk over them. Use a clean towel, dip into the mixture and then pat very gently on your burned areas.

Do this for 10–15 minutes and then take a cool shower where

you will not—we repeat not—rub on any of the burned areas. The milk contains lactic acid, which immediately will seep into your pores and reduce any swelling. Meanwhile, the proteins from the milk and the fat will naturally moisturize your skin and even prevent it from coming off in the next few days.

peppermint pain relief (for sunburn)

We have been hearing lately that 15 minutes of unprotected sun exposure is a health benefit for women because it gives us a quick infusion of vitamin D. But the trouble with this notion is that we don't want sunburned skin from getting a little too much exposure. We have a natural cure for sunburn from Dorie Byers, RN, author of *Natural Beauty Basics* that will help you say "ahhhhh."

1   **cup distilled water**
¼   **cup dried or ½ cup fresh peppermint leaves**

Boil water and then add the peppermint. Cover your pot and allow this to simmer for 15 minutes. Strain the water into a mug or bowl and throw out the peppermint.

Now, fill a tub with lukewarm water and pour in the peppermint water. Repeat this bath another time or two or three for relief.

Beauty Tip

Shhhhh…It happens to all of us. It's laundry day and there isn't a fresh towel to be found in the bathroom. Don't reach for the slightly damp towel from last night because it could be harboring bacteria. Instead, you can grab a fresh cotton T-shirt and your hair will actually thank you for it. Hair pros know that a cotton T-shirt will absorb the water from your hair while not allowing it to frizz. You might wish for it to be laundry day seven days a week now!

Just soak for 20 minutes and relax as your burn feels better.

You can also use lavender mint or lemon mint. An added benefit is that you will smell minty fresh after your bath.

southern sweet potato face

There is truth to the term "Southern Beauty." These ladies have that extra special something when it comes to having vibrant, smooth and young-looking skin. When we interviewed them, they slyly told us it was due to their taste for... sweet potato pie. It's not just that they actually eat sweet potato everything, but they also use the orange spud as a mask for their gorgeous faces.

Sweet potatoes are a significant source of vitamin A and beta-carotene, both rich in antioxidants and very nourishing for the skin. Many dermatologists believe beta-carotene jump-starts the production of new skin cells and also helps to keep the surface area of skin soft, smooth, and resilient.

Beauty Tip

You're down to the bottom of that tube of lotion and ready to toss it in the garbage. Stop. Resist the urge to purge! Take out a clean scissors and cut open the bottom of the tube. There can be days of product still available stuck to the bottom.

Our friends at *Beautiful Living: Balance & Joy* magazine created a wonderful recipe for a sweet potato facial treatment that is second to none. By the way, bake another sweet potato for a low-calorie lunch. Add a little cinnamon on top to balance your blood sugar, and you will also have a great diet meal.

1–2 ounces cooked mashed sweet potatoes
1 tablespoon oats (oatmeal)
1 tablespoon of honey
Pinch of nutmeg

Mix all of the ingredients together to form a thick paste. Adjust the ingredients, if needed, to make thinner. Add water to make it thinner. Add oats for a thicker consistency.

Apply to the face and neck. Leave on for five minutes. Tissue off the bulk, rinse with warm water, and gently pat dry skin.

LYDIA CORNELL'S NATURAL BEAUTY SECRETS

Lydia Cornell was second only to Farrah in the '80s when it came to a blonde bombshell. The star of *Too Close for Comfort* is now a radio show host, author, and advocate of teenage girls. We asked this gorgeous beauty for a few of her natural beauty regimes from her kitchen.

- For hair protein to strengthen hair: Whip up a raw egg and olive oil and put the mixture on your hair. It strengthens your hair cuticle just like Keratin! Put your hair in a plastic bag and turban. Let it soak for at least an hour. Wash with moisturizing shampoo and cream rinse.

- Preparation H for a puffy face. I told a friend about it and one day he appeared

Beauty Tip

Laugh from your belly. That's right. If you're down (and out of it) then simply find something or someone who will give you a good, deep belly laugh. According to researchers at Osaka University in Japan, even watching a very funny movie was more effective at decreasing mental stress than watching a drama. That's because Chromogranin A is released and this is a great protein in the body that creates positive mental feelings and reduces negative stress. You can also check out a funny TV show, talk show, or even watch your child do something funny. Cute photos can also produce this effect. Place them around your house, so you can glance at them when you're feeing down and blue.

with Preparation H all over his face after a hangover. It takes down swelling and shrinks hemorrhoids.

- Hot luxurious bath with one cup Epsom salts, tablespoon of olive oil, vanilla flavoring, or splash of perfume (any kind you can spare.) This moisturizes your body, making it silky soft, and relaxes muscles.

- Cut up oranges and put the orange pieces by your bed or desk. It will wake you up.

- Vanilla is an aphrodisiac.

- Fresh rosemary plucked from the herb garden: break it and sniff it, and it perks up the brain.

- I make my own wrinkle cream. Crush a vitamin C tablet or buy dissolvable powdered vitamin C crystals (from Trader Joe's at $9.99 for a huge jar) or powdered "EmergenC" vitamin C packs. Mix one teaspoon of vitamin C with any inexpensive moisture face cream, vitamin E cream, or Palmer's Cocoa Butter Formula. This is as good as any expensive department store vitamin C cream that runs $40-$100. Vitamin C turns the cream dark, but that is good. It means it's working.

- Lemon squeezed on freckles or sunspots lightens them.

- Gargle with hydrogen peroxide to whiten teeth. We add a drop of peppermint extract for a mouthwash flavor.

slumdog perfect skin

Ever since *Slumdog Millionaire*, we have been obsessed with the gorgeous, flawless skin of the women of India. We had to find out their secret for not only youthful skin, but for their bright skin that shows no signs of discoloration or brown spots. Here is how they do it in India.

1   **tablespoon of turmeric powder**
1   **cup of plain yogurt**

Mix the turmeric powder with the yogurt. Apply to the skin. Leave on for 5–10 minutes. Rinse off with warm water.

You will have brighter skin in a short period of time by using this potent India spice.

bright eyes on no sleep

Last night you tossed and turned, and twisted around more times than a Cirque du Soleil performer. Insomnia is bad enough, and one of the worries attached to it is how you will look the next day. We have a quick makeup-artist tip that will make even the puffiest eyes look better on almost zero sleep. It's all in the mascara. In order to look "faux bright-eyed," simply coat your top and bottom lashes with one swipe of mascara. Then return to the middle of your top lashes and add another coat of mascara only to the center portion of your lashes. Believe us, it's better than a cup of strong coffee.

clumps have us in the dumps

It never fails: You finally find a mascara you love, but then after several uses it seems to get dry and clumpy instead of smooth and easy to use. The save is in your fridge. Take out a can of Coca-Cola and put exactly one drop of it into your mascara. That sugary syrup will break up the mascara without turning it into a runny, watery mess.

BLUE PLATE SPECIALS: BEAUTY COOKBOOK RESCUES ON THE LOWEST BUDGET POSSIBLE

hot lashes

It's finally date night with your significant other, but in these economically challenging times there wasn't room in the budget for a new little black dress or even the latest lip-gloss that is in all the magazines. You want to do something now that says wow—for little to no cost. Here's a tip: In your bathroom, take out your blow dryer and your eyelash curler. Turn your blow dryer on medium hot and give your curler a shot of heat for 15 seconds. Now, use your "curling iron-esque" eyelash curler on your lashes. They will curl perfectly and the heat will set in the dramatic, flirty eye look for the entire night. Cost: Zero.

head case

From the Beauty Cookbook Bureau in India comes a way to feel beautiful and de-stress at the same time. The gorgeous ladies there include a do-it-yourself scalp massage in their grooming routines. The idea is to get your circulation jump-started while removing the frown from your face because you're erasing tension—and also preventing fine lines from forming. An added benefit of a scalp massage is that it helps stimulate your hair follicles and makes your hair shinier, sleeker, and even promotes hair growth if you're losing too much of it down the shower.

We also know ladies who over-process their hair with dye, which creates breakage. The following massage helped new hair grow in ...and fast. Now, here is what you do: Use a firm touch with your clean fingertips and make small circles all over your scalp, forehead, and temples. Alternate from the top of your noggin, down to your forehead, over to your temples, and then even down your face to the bottom of your neck. Make sure to concentrate on both the front and back of your head. Take 10 minutes and do this daily, even if you have to lock yourself in the bathroom. If you put on some soothing music, then you're relaxing to the hilt. Cost: Zero.

cover me

You gotta love a beauty tip that gives you permission to do something that makes you feel a little guilty in the first place. That's why we love research that shows that five minutes of extra sleep in the morning increases your levels of the hormone serotonin. Known as the "feel-good" juice in your body, it also makes you relax, look happy, and thus look even more beautiful. We say that five minutes is nice, but we're upping the beauty ante here and insisting that you give yourself an extra 10 minutes snuggled into your pillow. By the way, the research also shows that sleeping a little later in the morning gives you more of a mood-enhancing hit than going to bed early at night. Cost: Zero

FOURTH COURSE *sexy body recipes*

hot chocolate bath

4	**tablespoons unsweetened cocoa**
1	**cup of milk**
½	**cup unscented bubble bath**

Did you know that you can actually take a dip in your hot chocolate, and your skin will thank you for it?

Simply combine the cocoa, milk, and bubble bath and then mix.

Pour this sweet-smelling concoction into your warm bath water near the faucet in order to achieve maximum bubbles.

Sink into the tub, but don't drink it, which will be tempting because it smells so delicious. By the way, the cocoa powder and milk contain natural exfolients, so you'll have skin

Beauty Tip

Victoria doesn't know this bust-enhancing secret. No offense to Victoria because we love all of her secrets, but we have a great way to live that childhood chant, "We must, we must, we must increase our bust." Simply take a blush brush and put a bit of bronzer on it. Now trace that bronzer over your inner breast curves. Finish by putting a little shimmer (even a dab of extra virgin olive oil) between your breasts. Viola! You instantly look like you've had work done… for little to no work!

smoother than you could ever imagine.

Try this with your significant other to learn the meaning of real hot chocolate.

body bubbly

1   cup of sugar
1   cup of yogurt
¼   cup of the champagne of your choice

This is a great sexy spa recipe that serves a dual purpose. You will use a little bubbly for this scrub and then you can drink the rest for a romantic night with your significant other. The last part is up to you, but we can give you the recipe for the beauty portion of the evening. Mix the sugar into the yogurt and then add the champagne. Run a warm shower and step inside with your mate. You will gently rub this mixture on each other to create the softest, smoothest results. The cultures in the yogurt, combined with the scrubbing power of sugar will get rid of any and all dead skin cells. The bonus is that the antioxidants in the champagne (or any kind of grapes) help to instantly repair any skin damage. We suggest a nice ice bucket on the bathroom counter with two crystal flutes, two big white fluffy robes, and your imagination for the rest of your sexy spa night for two. Just don't blame us if this becomes a regular date night event.

Beauty Tip

At any age, line your lips with a nude liner to create shape and keep your gloss within your lip line.

sexy, soft lips

We love gorgeous hair and dewy faces, but a secret beauty weapon is staring right back at you in the mirror. It's your lips. They can make a pretty face gorgeous, and even a tired one ultra-sexy. Frankly, we're tired of the tire-inflated Hollywood look, and prefer healthy, moist, and soft lips. Here is how you can get them:

1   **warm wash cloth**
1   **teaspoon of honey**

Take a warm washcloth and rub gently over lips to exfoliate.

Take a dollop of honey out of the jar. (The cream honey in a jar available in health food stores is easiest to use).

Layer the honey over the lips while you sleep and wake up in the morning to a smooth, soft, supple mouth. (Please don't blame us for the sticky pillow case. This is a night to use your best from Target.)

Beauty Tip

Your lips have more lines on them and feel rougher as you age, so they require a little TLC on a daily basis. Make sure to always buy lipstick with an SPF factor in it, or put a little sunscreen under your lipstick before you leave the house. One warning: Super shiny lip gloss actually makes your lips more attractive to the sun, so make sure to put the higher SPF cream underneath your lip gloss to avoid burned, dried-up, chapped lips. A few swipes a day with your lip balm is another great lip saver. We also love a little bit of lip exfoliation at night with a damp washcloth. Gently run the cloth over your lips, and then finish with a repair-friendly lip cream or a little Vasoline or honey to get that kisser in better shape.

natural breast firmer

We've just gone through an era of big, fake, over-sized breasts, and now women are saying a B or C cup is enough. Can we say that expectations are deflating? Even Hollywood celebrities are opting to get their breast implants removed for fashion, health, or self-esteem reasons. Now, women just want to enjoy the real thing and go *au naturale*, but that doesn't mean you have to settle for sagging, loose, or drooping boobs. We have a secret way to keep the "girls" perky, upward, and firm.

1   **teaspoon of vitamin E oil**
1   **tablespoon of yogurt**
1   **egg**

Mix the above ingredients together in a bowl and then massage this mixture onto breasts.

Wear an old bra over the mixture for at least twenty minutes. Rinse off with warm water.

Hellooooooo, girlfriends!

Beauty Tip

Before applying red lipstick, put a tiny bit of Vaseline on your front-teeth to keep the color away.

Beauty Tip

If it's that time of the day (or year) to shave your legs, there is the added problem of those little red bumpy things that seem to pop up on your gams after a nice, close shave. The problem is, your legs are dry, and you're literally ripping the hair out with a razor. To beat red bumpies, just jump in the shower or tub and give yourself a few minutes for your legs to get wet and soft, and to get your pores to open up. Use a new razor to shave. The bumps won't appear because you're shaving soft skin and not tough skin that's resisting the process and having a bumpy reaction.

the drink is on you: margarita salt body rub

1   **cup fine sea salt**
2   **oz. olive oil**
     The juice of one lime
¾   **oz. white tequila**

Think of this as a toast to your beautiful body because the basic margarita makes an excellent natural body scrub. The lime and tequila are antiseptics that detox your skin and help improve tone and texture.

Just combine the sea salt, olive oil, lime juice, and tequila in a plastic bottle.

Jump into the shower and rub the mixture onto your damp skin in small circles. If you want the salt to be a little softer than just add more oil to your mixture.

hot legs

2   **tablespoons salt**
2   **tablespoons baking soda**
     Juice of one lemon

Mix the salt, balking soda, and the juice of one lemon and bring into

Beauty Tip

You're frantic because your date is waiting. You reach for that new bottle of fancy foundation that you just splurged on at the department store. What were you thinking when you purchased this too-dark gunk? Instead of allowing pure panic to set in (panic causes fine lines!), just grab your sunscreen—especially the kind with zinc oxide in it. Pour a bit of foundation into your palm and then lighten it by using one drop, and then two or three drops of sunscreen. Each drop of sunscreen will make a difference, so go slowly until you create your own personal foundation with a very good SPF level.

Another great trick is to just mix a little moisturizer into the bottom of too-dark foundation. You won't use it as your base anymore, but you've just created a wonderful liquid bronzer for that sun-kissed glow.

the shower with you. Rub the mixture on your damp legs. Then rinse.

The salt is a gentle exfolient that gets an even better punch when mixed with the citric acid in a lemon and the slightly alkaline properties of baking soda. This treatment will adjust the PH of your skin and result in a satin feeling.

sweet body bailout

Your favorite shampoo
1   box of granulated sugar

Beauty Tip

No time for a teeth whitener? Try eating some abrasive vegetables like broccoli. They're a natural stain lifter.

Mix equal parts shampoo and granulated sugar for a cheap and natural body scrub.

The beauty of this is you can change the fragrance of the scrub by choosing a different shampoo. You will not only enjoy the scrub part, but the shampoo will foam up and act as a cleanser. The end result is your skin will be super soft and smooth, but without using any oil.

whipped cream body extravaganza

It's sexy, silly, and fun. Whipped cream makes Jell-O, fruit, and brownies look, feel, and taste so much better. And guess what? It will do the same thing for your skin. Even though she didn't have tubs of low-fat Cool Whip during her heyday, even Cleopatra was a big proponent of milk baths, and this follows along the same lines because cream is just a thicker form of milk. Cleo knew that fresh cream was extremely beneficial to the skin because it contains protein and lactic acids that soften and moisturize the skin, while making it look softer, younger, and dewy. Did we also mention the word sexy?

1   cup of fresh heavy cream

Whisk the fresh cream until soft peaks form and it has a soft and fluffy consistency.

Lather the cream all over your body as if you were icing a cake. You can include your hair. Leave on for 5 to 10 minutes. Rinse off in warm bath.

By the way, this is also a fun, sexy couples activity for a quiet night of moisturizing at home!

don't sweat it (anymore)

Black tea
A washcloth

Brew a batch of black tea, but don't drink it. Let it cool and then saturate a washcloth. Place the compress under each arm for five minutes.

Do this every night for two weeks and the tannic acid in the tea will permanently reduce your sweat production.

Beauty Tip

Forget expensive toothpaste for whiter teeth. Do what your grandmother used to do to get those pearly white. Just grab a little bit of baking soda from the kitchen and use it as your toothpaste. It will naturally whiten your choppers.

Beauty Tip

Do you ever wonder how the stars always have thick eyelashes? Yes, they have individual fake lashes put on by makeup pros, but you can come close to that effect at home with your own drugstore mascara. Just think about your school days! First, look up to the heavens while taking the wand of your mascara and putting it at the base of your lashes. Move the brush through your lashes in a Z shape. Two coats should make it appear as if you just dismissed your makeup artist and had falsies put on.

chocolate sexy body butter

You want to spice things up at home, and you know the way to your man's heart is through his senses…and we mean his nose. If your significant other loves chocolate (and who doesn't?), then we have a great way to get romantic in the sweetest way possible. Why not try a cocoa body butter to really stir up his senses?

2   **tablespoons grated cocoa butter**
2   **tablespoons caster oil**
2   **tablespoons vodka**

Mix the cocoa butter and castor oil together in a warm plate in the microwave. Add vodka and stir till a creamy texture.

Allow to cool, and layer on the body. Rinse off later in a sexy shower or nibble some off his shoulder.

va va vanilla

It's your anniversary, a first date, or a second honeymoon, and you've decided to bake a cake. (How sweet—pun intended). The problem is, all that Betty Crocker-ing is taking forever. So when are you going to primp for your honey? We can save you a few minutes by suggesting that you grab the vanilla extract from the cake recipe and use it on you!

Beauty Tip

Don't feel guilty about a warm cup of hot-chocolate this winter because you're saving your skin with each sip. The flavanols in the hot chocolate are known to get the redness out of your skin by 25 percent, and plump your skin by 28 percent. Research indicates that the flavanols get rid of skin irritations, and they also ramp up the flow of healing blood to your skin cells naturally. If you're not in the mood for something hot, then a few bites of dark chocolate will also do the same trick. You can thank us later. (But remember, we said a few bites—not a truckload of candy bars!)

Simply dab the vanilla behind your ears, on the crook of your inner arms, and in the V between your breasts. You can even use a bit of it behind your kneecaps.

For centuries, the scent of vanilla was considered an aphrodisiac. According to the Smell and Taste Research Institute, the scent of vanilla sexually arouses men.

Oh, don't forget to take your cake out of the oven. Nothing like the smell of burned pastries to overpower the vanilla. Have a sweet night!

Beauty Tip

Did you know that, according to a University of Rochester study, men are more attracted to women wearing red clothing than other colors? Ruby lipstick or red nail polish will also cause men to feel that zing for you. The attraction is rooted in the, uh, nether regions. It turns out some of our female simian ancestors turned red when they were willing to hit the sheets.

naked ride body smoother

This is called the Lady Godiva Scrub, because even when you're naked, the only thing anyone will be looking at is your noble glow. Lady Godiva was a full-figured beauty and the wife of Earl Leofic of Mercia. She was known for asking her very powerful and rich husband to give tax breaks to the people of Coventry. He agreed—with one little caveat: He would charge these peasants *less* if she would ride through town naked. (At least he couldn't be accused of being an over-possessive husband!)

Being a woman who believed in community service, Lady Godiva simply told everyone to please stay indoors, and then she took her naked ride with only her long hair as a cover-up. There are rumors that she went through a few beauty rituals before getting on that horse, even though they didn't have *The Insider* in those days. Try this one for your own naked strut through your condo or home:

¼   **cup granulated sugar**
2   **tablespoons light vegetable oil**
2   **table spoons fresh whole milk**

Mix ingredients together to form a cream. Before bathing, gently rub the mixture all over your body to increase circulation and remove dry or flaking skin.

Rinse your body with warm water and moisturize as usual.

take two aspirins and call to thank us in the morning

Even the best beauty regimes, including perfect plucking and wonderful waxing, can produce unwanted irritation and itchy little bumps. What do you do when your skin rebels and looks worse than the hair that was there in the first place? The worry is no reason to allow your body to go Grizzly Adams. If you're plucking out unwanted hairs, then have this recipe on hand for the aftermath to ensure that your skin stays baby pink. Read on for a quick cure for bikini waxing traumas, or, as we like to call them, "Things that go bump under our Victoria's Secret."

2   **aspirin**
    A few drops of water
    Tea Tree Oil

Crush the aspirin between two spoons and then add a few drops of water until it has the consistency of grade-school paste.

Rub the paste on any areas where you just plucked and let it dry. Aspirin is a natural anti-inflammatory and will prevent any red spots or bumps from forming because the little pill halts the production of prostaglandins (unsaturated fatty acids secreted by cells that cause the problem in the first place).

Now, if your trouble involves a bikini wax that creates little red bumps, then please don't buy expensive lotions to combat the problem. For a few dollars at a natural store, you can buy a small bottle of tea tree oil.

Lightly coat the area that was just waxed. The healing oil will prevent those annoying bumps from showing up in the morning.

go directly to glow, collect 200 compliments

You can go directly to a high-priced department store and invest upwards to fifty dollars in special oils from the "rainforest"—those exotic elixirs designed to give you a sexy and shimmering evening glow. At The Beauty Cookbook HQ, we find that a recipe for a very high credit card bill. But never fear: we found the same results for under five dollars. It's a little bit of regular old Johnson's Baby Oil that might already be in your nursery or bathroom and that smells absolutely amazing. Top makeup artists tell us the key is not to use too much—or cover too many body areas with your new instant "glow." Instead just put a few small dots of oil in the palm of your hand and rub on your arms, shins, or over your upper chest area. The goal is to have subtle shimmer without looking like you're about to hit the beach. Think oil in moderation and not oil slick.

strawberry feet forever

5   **strawberries**
1   **tablespoon kosher salt**
1   **tablespoon of essential oils**

With a fork, smash the strawberries, but don't make them too smooth. You want them to work as an exoliant.

Add the salt and oil to the mixture. Place the mixture on a warm washcloth and run over any calloused spots on your feet. Your tootsies should be silky smooth and most of the tough spots gone when you're done. This is fun to do to your mate—and vice versa!

hand it to me

You've been in the kitchen making that amazing shrimp dish for your new boyfriend or significant other, but then you realize that your idea of a romantic dinner is now severely challenged by the fact that your hands smell like you've been working on a fish dock all day long. There's nothing sexy about smelling fishy. You've already taken your shower and done your hair, so that isn't an option. A quick smell remover: A lemon. Cut it in half and rub the juice onto your hands. The smell will become a memory. Lemons can also help get rid of dry skin because the acid vitamin C combo in them will help get rid of dry skin and promote healing.

vanilla honey tubbie

If you're having a frazzled type of day, let us just say three words to you: <u>vanilla honey bath</u>. Don't you feel better already? This one is a great romantic-couples recipe, too. Just fill the bathroom with some vanilla scented candles, dim the lights, create this sexy bath and then put on a little music. The bathroom will smell like heaven and the honey in the tub will certainly please your real honey.

½ **cup honey**
½ **cup of your favorite liquid soap**
1 **teaspoon pure vanilla**

Mix the above ingredients in a squeeze bottle. Run a bath of warm water and slowly squeeze half a cup of this mixture under the faucet as you run the water. Make sure to shake your bottle a few times before using because the honey will settle on the bottom. When your bath foams up and fills up, you're ready for one of the most beautifully scented nights of your life.

You should keep the rest of the mixture in the fridge 'cause you can use it for two weeks after the initial mixing.

FIFTH COURSE
forty years young recipes

e-i-e-i-o facial

Prevent wrinkles around the mouth with a daily facial exercise. Make an exaggerated "O" and "E" as if you were saying (EEEEEOOOOO) with your mouth for 30 seconds. Purse your lips right, center, and then left. Hold each movement for 30 seconds. Repeat. Then stick your tongue out as far as you can while keeping your eyes wide. This exercise relaxes your facial and jaw muscles. Tension in these areas will make you look older, but once you relax then you will not only shave off the years, but also look kinder.

brown makes us frown

The juice of one lemon
½   **cup plain soy yogurt**
3   **strawberries**

Over the years, we've had so many calls and letters from ladies who fret about brown patches on their faces. We feel your pain and now it's time to make what's causing you to develop frown lines (the horror) fade into the sunset. This is a once a month treatment because it's powerful. You will take three strawberries, the juice of one lemon and ½ cup plain soy yogurt and mix it in your blender or food processor. Chill in your fridge for half an hour. Take the mixture and apply it to your face, neck, and even your chest area or other parts of your body that contain brown spots. You will leave this mask on for half an hour. The strawberries give you a powerful dose of vitamin-C to tighten pores, while the soy yogurt is a great natural way of fading brown spots on the body. Please stay out of the sun for the next day because your skin will be a little bit sensitive and might burn easily.

puffy eye rx

1   chilled spoon
Cotton balls
Milk

You had a late night either having fun (we hope) or working on a big report, and you woke up with puffy eyes. To reduce those bags, place either a chilled spoon that you keep in the freezer on your eye area, or soak cotton balls with chilled milk. Rest either of them on your eye area and feel the puff go down in about five minutes.

make-a-molehill-out-of-a-mountain zit zapper

This is perfect for the angst-and-pimple ridden teen in your life, or for those of us over 40 going through hot flashes and acne at the same time—list under the category of "Life Is Not Fair."

1   **package dry yeast**
2   **tablespoons water**
2   **drops from a fresh lemon**

Open the package of yeast and pour it into a bowl. Add two tablespoons of water, one drop at a time—mixing well after you add each drop. Your goal is to make an even paste where all of the yeast is dissolved and not chalky.

After your water is gone and mixed, then add two drops from a fresh lemon. Stir well. Put a dab of this mixture on every zit.

By the end of the day your mountain should be a molehill. (Special thanks to skin care guru Sonya Dakar for this one!)

soy hand soak

You look down one day post-40 and realize, "I really need new shoes, and, gosh, my hands look sort of old." Blame dishes, showering, and the effects of pollution as a few of the reasons why the thin skin on hands ages rapidly. We have a quick recipe that you can do all the time as a relaxing skin-softening treat for your tired and overworked hands. This will also help smooth the skin and reduce the appearance of lines and wrinkles.

Beauty Tip

We want to give you the best tips for not only what to put on your skin, but also what to put in your body as well to ensure fabulous skin. Did you know that research shows that soy may help protect against the sun's photo-aging damage? One study, published in the European Journal of Nutrition, reported that a soy-based supplement with ingredients including vitamins, fish protein, and extracts from white tea, grape seed, and tomato, improved the skin's structure and firmness after just six months. Grab some soy, tomatoes, and red wine and you will soon be bouncing quarters off your face. Okay, not that we want loose change flying at you, but….

1   **bowl of warm water**
½   **cup soy milk**
1   **cap full of bubble bath or liquid
    soap in some yummy flavor**

Place the cap full of bubble bath on the bottom of the bowl and then fill the bowl with warm water.

Heat the soy milk in the microwave just to take the chill off of it, but don't make it too hot. You don't want to burn yourself. Add the soy milk to the water. Soak your hands for 10 minutes.

When you're done, dry them, but leave them a little bit moist before applying your favorite moisturizer.

The soy has antioxidants in it, which will make your skin glow and feel silky, while the moisturizer will sink in deeply because your pores are still open. Enjoy this treatment whenever you need a quick get-away-from-it-all spa treatment at home.

Beauty Tip

It's important to keep your posture straight and strong, especially after 40 when calcium levels drop. As the years pass, women often begin to slouch and hunch at the shoulders. An easy way to straighten up is to grab a kitchen broom or mop. Instead of wiping away spilled OJ, take the broom and hold it horizontally behind your back. Gently lift up. This move strengthens the rhomboids, which are the muscles that connect the shoulder blades to the spine. This will also correct the tendency to round the upper spine forward.

get-rid-of-wrinkles secret potion

There is one ingredient that we keep coming across to help get rid of fine lines and wrinkles—the little green grape. Many of the hottest, most expensive creams and potions on the market have some form of grapeseed lotion or oil as the top ingredient. We talked to several beauty experts and they agree that grapes are great for wrinkles! It almost sounds too simple, but here's a recipe for fighting aging on your face.

2–3   large green grapes

Cut the grapes in half and gently crush the inner mushy part on your face and neck. Make sure that you get the "crows feet" and the lines around your mouth.

Leave this on your face and let it set for 20 minutes. Rinse with cool water and pat dry.

hot, not so much

It is always good to look hot, be hot, and think you are hot, but when you really are hot from menopause, it's not so sexy. It's uncomfortable, and it usually comes with the charming combo platter of water retention, irritability and night sweats. Most women dread menopause, but it's a natural part of aging, with symptoms that can be alleviated with a few simple tricks. In fact, the women of France have taken the overheated problem into their own hands to come up with this kitchen cure. All you need is sage. This herb has natural estrogen that will help balance hormones, and the tannins in it help stop the sweating. You can grow sage in your own garden, or simply buy it in your grocery or health food store. A good way to use sage is to

Beauty Tip
Did you know that your fingernails grow 25 percent faster these days than when your grandmother was young? Thank the protein-rich diets that most of us women consume, including chicken, fish and nuts. The University of North Carolina recently did a study comparing nail and toe nail growth rates with a 1938 survey. In the late '30s, adult women ate a carb filled diet of bread and potatoes. Women who smoke (as many did in 1938) have much slower nail growth rates, too, than ladies in 2009.

Beauty Tip
Eating sage will also help stop underarm perspiration.

sprinkle it on your salads and over your veggies. It's also delicious baked into chicken or on fish.

midnight wanderer skin secret

There are many wonderful things about hitting the big "4-Oh"—but one of them is not your bladder being on full alert overnight and that new 3 a.m. trip to your bathroom spa. We can't argue with Mother Nature when it comes to our pipes, but we can turn the trip into a beauty booster. You're up anyway, so reapply a little bit of moisturizer to your face. We guarantee that as your pipes age, your mug will look younger and younger by this "extra" dose of moisture each day...or should we say night? Hey, us "over 40s" need all the "boosters" we can get.

sun-kissed smoothie

1   **small handful of dry short grain rice**
1   **tablespoon of honey**
1   **teaspoon pomegranate juice**

In small circles and with a gentle hand, rub the rice over your face for two minutes. Dry with a towel.

Mix the honey and pomegranate juice and moisturize your face with the mixture. Allow it to dry on your face for 15 minutes. Wash again.

This will give your skin an instant freshening glow.

quick shopping guide for over-40 beauty

DID YOU KNOW?

At the meat-counter: The good: lean beef. The better: organic beef. The best: grass-fed beef. The latter has much less fat, but can be a tough chew and also expensive. Make sure you marinate it to soften and tenderize before cooking.

In the produce section: The good: romaine. The better: watercress. The best: spinach. Spinach is rich in iron, which delivers oxygen to your cells. This is key to slowing down the aging process.

In the egg section. The good: packaged egg whites. The better: whole eggs. The best is Omega-3 fortified eggs. The latter has the nutrients of regular eggs, plus up to 300 mg of fatty acids in each one. If you don't get enough fish in your diet, just add these eggs.

tea, no sympathy facial

1   cup green tea (brewed)
1   tablespoon plain yogurt
½   teaspoon cornstarch

Brew the tea and leave a cup for you to sip (it's good for you!), and use just one tablespoon for your facial. Mix that with the yogurt and cornstarch.

Chill this mixture in the fridge for 20 minutes. Smooth it on your face and relax for 15 minutes.

This facial will calm your skin and leave it even toned with a youthful glow. It will also attack the free radicals that age the skin.

tomato face

Several thin slices of tomatoes
The other half of that tomato

Think of this as a two-step "gravy" facial—at least that's what "The Sopranos" called a tomato topping. You can create an amazing weekly facial that will get rid of pimples and redness by starting with thin tomato slices.

Place them on your face and relax for 15 minutes. Yes, we said do nothing but close your eyes and let the tomato juice sink into your pores.

Before you wash your face, grab the other half of the tomato. Using the smooth skin side, rub small circles all over your face. You will finish by rinsing with warm water.

This treatment works because the lycopene in the tomatoes naturally declogs your pores while working as a powerful astringent to ward off the bacteria that causes pimples. The facial massage with the second part of the tomato helps with circulation and allows the juices to penetrate even deeper. Your pores will be glad that you skipped one salad and used a tomato for beauty!

figs for fine lines

Figs are the ugly stepsister of papayas and pineapples. They're stars, however, when it comes to ridding the skin of surface impurities and dead skin. It's true that these little wrinkled fruits don't look all that attractive, but the little "old man," that dark and dull fig, is actually a potent fighter of fine lines and wrinkles for women. Figs also have high enzyme content, so don't use them on your gorgeous face for any longer than five minutes.

1   fresh fig

Cut the fig in half and turn the halves inside out. Scrape the inside flesh into a bowl, and mash until smooth.

Spread mixture onto clean face. Let sit for five minutes. Rinse with cool water.

chef's surprise: beauty shockers that really work

You're Hot and You're Cold: You're exhausted after a long day and can't even find the strength or resolve to moisturize. We feel your pain. The solution, or quick pick-me-up, is in your shower. Jump in and spend 30 seconds in warm water, followed immediately by 30 seconds in cool water. (Colder if you can take it!) The hot and then cold beauty treatment is an ancient one, and it not only perks up your entire system, but tightens your post-40 pores.

Pepper Por Favor: So your nose is puffy and a little red in the morning thanks to allergies or a bit of a cold coming on. What to do? Take a dollop of cleansing cream in your hand and add one quick shake of black pepper. Now wash around your nose area. The pepper will gently open your closed nasal passages and clear them up—at least for a little while. Just don't forget to put the pepper back in the kitchen, because later on your husband might wonder what the heck it's doing in the bathroom.

Scotch...and Shadow: You just splurged on that gorgeous eggplant-colored eye shadow, but went a bit too far when you were applying it to your eyelids. Now, it's raining purple flecks onto your cheeks and you've already applied your foundation. How do you remove the flecks without taking off your base coat? Easy. Keep a little bit of Scotch tape in the bathroom. Carefully take a little piece of tape, wrap it around your finger sticky side out, and gently touch the shadow that went astray. It will attach to the tape without removing any other makeup.

SIXTH COURSE *spa recipes*

pina colada pampering

Want to get tropical, but can't afford the airfare to an island? You can make it a spa night at home with a few simple ingredients.

1   **fresh coconut**
    Your favorite unscented body cream

Split open a fresh coconut and pour the milk into a small bowl. Add a scoop of your favorite unscented body cream. Grab your whisk and whip up this concoction until it feels very fluffy.

Massage it into your skin for a tropical spa treatment that will leave you feeling soft and smelling yummy. The smell will linger into the next day, so don't be surprised if friends ask you about your new "perfume."

Beauty Tip

To boost your metabolism, draw a hot bath and add a cup of Epsom salts. You will be releasing trapped fats because the magnesium in the salt comes right through your pores and lowers the cortisol levels in your bloodstream. Remember that this is the hormone that helps keep the fat in place. All of the above will give yourr metabolism a nice kick-start.

BCB EXPERT: DEREK HOFMANN, DIRECTOR OF THE SPA AT FOUR SEASONS HOTEL LOS ANGELES AT BEVERLY HILLS

At the swanky Four Seasons in Beverly Hills, the to-die-for spa offers relaxation, distraction, and de-stressing. Their beauty and wellness treatments are second to none, and some are hard to duplicate at home (it is tough to exfoliate your own back!). Derek Hofmann was kind enough to help us figure out the principles and products that you can use to re-create the experience of a celeb hotspot called The Spa.

Derek also provided us with some body basics as a primer for newbies to home skin care.

BODY

With strappy dresses, bikini season, and after-parties, everyone in Beverly Hills is looking for supple, silky, beautiful skin. The goal here is soft, smooth, hydrated skin, and an even tone and appearance. The basic steps you'll need to get there are exfoliation and moisturizing. We see best results from an invigorating exfoliation (scrub) and application of a great body moisturizer. Both of these steps offer you many options, as outlined below.

- *Exfoliation*: Salt, sugar, ground walnut shells, etc… basically something "abrasive." You'll be looking to slough of dull, dry, dead skin. You'll want whatever you're using to be moderately fine so that it moves well over the skin without scratching it.

- *Carrier Agent for Scrub*: Oil (body oil, olive oil, body cream, shea butter, etc). You'll mix the scrub with the carrier of your choice to create a glide over the skin.

- *Moisturizer*: Choose your favorite body oil, cream, butter, soufflé…whatever you love. We recommend something "clean" if not pure and organic. Your skin will drink this in so it should be great!

- *Method*: By using this homemade scrub on the entire body (not face) you'll be sloughing away dull, dead, dry skin as well as increasing circulation, and stimulating lymph function—all great for detoxification. You'll increase the appearance of your skin by stimulating the elimination of toxins and water for a more even appearance. You'll also be getting rid of dry patches and dull skin. The result is smooth and soft to the touch.

- *How Much*: Twice a week (tops) is all you'll need here. Follow the scrub with your moisturizer and you're done. Use the moisturizer daily, or every other day as needed.

Beauty Tip

Skin can be exfoliated with a blend of salt, essential oils of lime, orange, apple, and tangerine, tequila, and sunflower oil. After you're rinsed clean, grab a partner and try a massage using tequila and sage oil. Both tequila and sage are antiseptics making them perfect for cleansing and detoxifying the body. This treatment is specifically designed to improve circulation, help with digestion, and relieve fatigue.

margarita salt scrub with punta mita tequila massage

1   **cup fine sea salt**
2   **ounces olive oil**
    The juice of one lime
½   **shot (half ounce) of white tequila**

Mix all of the above ingredients in a bowl until blended. Slather this onto damp skin in gentle circular motions.

Scrubs are best performed at home in the tub or shower. This scrub is rather abrasive—a thorough exfoliation, so go easy. Rinse and follow with your favorite moisturizer. (The Spa suggests one with cucumber for its cooling, calming properties.)

Massage Portion: Our body therapists will apply tequila topically to the lower back and soles of the feet—to be removed by warm towels. A full body massage using sage oil follows. Use long, fluid strokes when massaging. This technique promotes deep relaxation, improves circulation and aids in the body's natural detoxification process. Whether or not you're able to incorporate the massage portion, this exfoliation will keep your skin soft and hydrated, and it's appearance smooth. A weekly exfoliation will keep your skin looking its best and prepped for hydration (from your moisturizer). This treatment can be performed year round. Remember that massage is tricky to perform solo, and usually your partner is not qualified for the really therapeutic stuff. This is best left to the pros, but a little shoulder rub, or attention where you need it can help loosen you up—as well as elevate spirits and help you connect.

FACE

It's what we look at when conversing, the first thing we see, what we remember, what makes us unique, and yes, unfortunately, people judge the book by its cover. So this one is probably the most important to get right. The spa strongly recommends putting your face in the hands of professionals first, and as often as needed.

Aestheticians are specifically and uniquely trained to address skin conditions and suggest solutions. You're best bet is to visit a qualified aesthetician and communicate your goals. You're aesthetician will not only give you a great facial specific to your complexion, but also lots of knowledge to take with you. Ask them about recommended products for your skin and ask them to be specific. You don't (always) need to buy the entire range. Have them customize a program for you. Any aesthetician worth their salt will work with you, your budget, and your lifestyle to tailor a program and home-care routine that will deliver your desired results.

HANDS AND FEET

Manicures and pedicures are considered routine maintenance to some, splurges and pampering to others, and often overlooked on a spa treatment menu. You notice, other people notice—we all notice!

You should keep your hands and feet smooth and moisturized (see exfoliation above). You can also buy a foot file or pumice and help keep calluses and rough spots away. Soak your feet in a warm bath. Keep hands moisturized between washings. All of these things are great ways to keep your fingers and toes in good shape between or instead of mani/pedis. There are tons of great lacquers on the market—so find your signature color or have fun dabbling!

You can usually schedule a "polish change" at your favorite spa or salon where they will shape your nails, condition the cuticles, and apply your polish at a much friendlier rate than a full service mani or pedi. This can help stretch the time between visits for your full manicure and pedicure—which will also stretch your hard-earned dollars a bit further.

HAIR AND SCALP

For most of us, this means shampoo, rinse, repeat—and then follow with a styling product. We offer a scalp treatment at The Spa, which consists of a hair and scalp oil application, warm towel treatment, and scalp massage. This is easy to do at home and doesn't take much time…and the results are great.

hair and scalp oil

Choose safflower oil, sesame seed oil, rapeseed oil, macadamia nut oil, avocado oil, olive oil—the list is endless. Add a few drops of sage essential oil.

Mix the oils and apply a small amount to your hair and scalp. Wrap in a warm towel or simply massage it into your scalp for as long as you choose to do it. You can shampoo this out after 15–30 minutes or leave it in overnight. Your hair and scalp will be nourished, moisturized, and toned. Massage stimulates circulation to your scalp. Sage oil is antimicrobial and antiviral. It can help improve greasy and oily hair by regulating sebum production of your scalp.

RANDOMS

Spas feel like a getaway, a sanctuary for a reason. At Four Seasons Los Angeles, our goal is a full sensory experience. I want the aromatherapy, the ambient music, the color schemes, the fabrics used, the tea, and infused water all to make a difference. You can do much of this at home as well.

Purchase a candle with pure essential oils or burn essential oils in a diffuser at home. Aromatherapy is a very powerful way to elevate your mood, induce relaxation, and promote clarity. Use different oils for different purposes. We use fabrics that feel good on the skin. From our robes, towels, and throws, to sheets and pillow covers. It feels good, you feel good = positive impact! Drink lots of water (you already know this one!). Enjoy the ritual of brewing, steeping, and drinking tea. A simple process, tea is a nice way to slow down, and it's good for you, too. Listen to music you enjoy. We choose selections that are rhythmic, soothing, inspiring, and ethereal at The Spa. We want to inspire reflection, rest, and peace. Our Relaxation Lounge, steam rooms, saunas, and showers are meant to encourage you to be quiet and still for as long as you like. Do this at home, too. Create a comfortable and quiet spot where you can relax and just be. Let go of stress—just let it go (really, just let it go).

Find what inspires you, makes you happy, makes and makes you feel good and follow that path. Take care of yourself (diet, exercise, de-stress) and choose what works for your personal beauty. Some people do it all; some people need only do very little. If you feel good, you look good… and often vice-versa.

the perfect manicure secret trick

1   **cotton ball**
1   **tablespoon of white vinegar**

Soak a cotton ball in one tablespoon of white vinegar. Rub this over your naked nails before you polish them. Let it dry.

Now it's time to do your regular manicure.

The mild acid in the vinegar will dry out any natural oil on your nails and make the polish stick in a way that it never has in the past. The polish will adhere to your nails and last for upwards of two weeks.

cool-it spa compress

Concentrated mint, lemon, or grapefruit essential oil
½   **gallon of water**

Add two drops of concentrated mint, lemon, or grapefruit essential oil into a half-gallon of water. Saturate a washcloth with the mixture, then ring it out, and create a roll with the cloth. Refrigerate the rolls.

When you're hot and sweaty after a long day, just unroll one of your "cool its" and place on your neck or forehead to cool your entire body.

RECIPES FOR THE SKIN BY GERI GIAGNORIO, THE SKIN TRAINER

quickie exfoliator

Baking soda will gently remove dead cell buildup and hydrogen, while peroxide is a natural bacteria fighter as well as a brightener. This is for all non-irritated skin types.

2   **tablespoons baking soda**
1   **tablespoon hydrogen peroxide**

Place both ingredients into the palm of one hand and mix together.

Using both hands, gently apply mixture directly to the skin. Using soft strokes, glide fingers over the face and neck, avoid eye area and nostrils.

Count quickly to twenty and rinse immediately. The hydrogen peroxide also carries one molecule of oxygen that will increase circulation and oxygen to the skin. It also carries anti-bacterial properties. This one will brighten and gently remove dead cell build-up with an easy one-two punch. Do this treatment once a week or every once in awhile when you feel your skin needs a little pick me up, but do not do more than once a week.

fast firming face masque

The masque is for all skin types. Men will especially love it after a shave.

1   egg
1   tablespoon of lecithin granules
2   whole aloe vera plant leaves

Combine all ingredients in a blender and process for 20 seconds or until creamy texture appears. Apply immediately to clean skin and leave on for 5–10 minutes. Relax for at least 5–10 minutes. Remove the masque with water.

Give yourself a gentle massage while removing it, and blend it into the neck and your chest.

This is a great refresher to the skin and body, but at the same time it helps to reduce inflammation and give a slight tightening to the skin. Aloe vera leafs left in their natural state (rind and gel) are great for in healing and firming the delicate tissues of the skin. You can do this treatment whenever you feel like it. Once or twice a week will give the skin a nice healthy and smooth glow.

aloe in ice

This is so simple and so beneficial to all skins. It's great anytime, but highly recommended first thing in the morning and after shaving, waxing, or anything that needs calming.

1   cup of pure aloe vera juice
1   aspirin (uncoated)
1   small cube ice tray

In a small pitcher, dissolve the aspirin in the aloe vera juice. Proceed to pour the aloe mixture in equal amounts into the cubes. Place the ice cube tray into the freezer.

Every morning, pop out an aloe ice cube and massage it all over the face and neck to refresh, hydrate, and nourish the skin first thing in the morning.

Beauty Tip

Here are our top five foods to eat to look like a star. Of course, it's hard to choose, but as far as hitting each area of the body, these foods will help the skin improve.

- *Kale and/or spinach everyday*
- *Broccoli sprouts*
- *Green apples*
- *Coconut water*

omega me masque

Protein, vitamins, lecithin and essential fatty acids all play a part in the health of the skin. Here's a way to instantly benefit your skin.

1	tablespoon of coconut oil
1	egg
1	tablespoon of ground flaxseed
½	avocado peeled and pitted

Combine all the ingredients in a blender until a creamy consistency appears. Apply immediately to skin and leave on for up to 10 minutes. Remove with a tissue and then rinse with warm water and finish with Aloe in Ice (recipe above) to really make your skin feel smooth, tight and glowing.

hot lips

Simple, easy, and eatable. Combine all the ingredients in a bowl and mix it up. It's that easy. Just apply and apply as much as you want.

1   teaspoon coconut oil
1   teaspoon of aloe vera gel
¼   teaspoon of Saigon Cinnamon
½   teaspoon of raw or clover honey
¼   teaspoon of any form of Stevia or a natural sugar substitute

Making your own lip treatment is fun and very easy, and what's better than all-natural ingredients on your lips? I mean really, you are going to be eating whatever is on your lips, so it better be good for you. This recipe is all natural and all good!

detoxing you from head to toe

Did you know that as you sleep, your body eliminates toxins—many of them through the skin? A nice, long, warm shower in the morning will help you wash them away, but we have a little extra beatifying tip for you…a DIY morning scrub from a chichi spa in NYC minus the hefty price tag! *Toxins be gone!*

½   cup brown sugar
½   cup oatmeal
1   cup olive oil
5   tablespoons line or lemon juice
    Lemon, lime or orange peel to add to the smell (optional)

Blend ingredients with a spatula. Use all over the body in the shower.

You can store the left-over mixture in the fridge for up to five days.

beauty drinks better than a cosmo

We're in awe of Paula Simpson, a top nutritionist and supplement formulator. Paula is a big proponent of juicing for great skin because it's a great way to ensure that you get your full servings of fruits and veggies. Why? Fruits and vegetables are naturally high in antioxidants, and antioxidants help to detoxify the body and boost the immune system. Nutrient-packed juices quickly provide essential antioxidants, vitamins and minerals that are essential for beautiful, glowing skin, hair, and nails.

A FEW TIPS FROM PAULA

When juicing with fruits and vegetables it's best to choose those that are richest in antioxidants and phytochemicals. Based on the Oxygen Radical Absorbance Capacity Scale, some of the best include:

- Garlic (supports a healthy immune system)

- Blueberries/Blackberries (source of fiber, proanthocyanidins, powerful water soluble antioxidants)

- Beets (supports healthy liver function)

- Spinach (source of iron, B vitamins, vitamin C; promotes collagen production, vitamins, and minerals)

- Strawberries (source of fiber, water soluble antioxidants)

- The cabbage family

- Kale (rich in calcium)

- Carrots (source of beta carotene and photo-protectant for skin)

- Tomatoes (source of lycopene and photo-protectant for skin)

- Apples (source of fiber, vitamin C; promotes collagen production)

health benefits of natural juices & broths

1. They are raw, therefore the nutrient density is not compromised.

2. They are quickly absorbed, so the juices are assimilated and absorbed much quicker than solid foods.

3. They're time efficient, so you can get super concentrated amounts of vital nutrients quickly and easily.

skin rejuvenator

4   carrots
1   celery stalk
1   tomato
½   beet with the greens
½   handful of wheatgrass
½   handful of parsley

Process all ingredients in juicer. Serve immediately.

This drink contains plenty of chlorophyll, beta carotene, vitamin C, flavonoids, and essential vitamins/minerals to nourish the skin from within.

energy regenerator

Here is a nutrient-dense, high-energy drink for those of you feeling sluggish or stressed. It's an excellent source of carotenoids, vitamin C, potassium, folic acid, magnesium, and phosphorus.

5   medium carrots, peeled and washed
¼   small head dark leafed cabbage, rinsed and drained
1   medium beet, scrubbed and cut into small chunks
4   celery stalks, washed

Core the cabbage and discard the white center. Cut into chunks. Process all vegetables in the juicer.

Serve immediately. Yields two servings.

cleansing berry

1   **apple**
½   **cup blackberries**
½   **cup blueberries**
½   **cup strawberries**
⅙   **teaspoon of honey**

Juice the fruits and put them in a shaker with the honey. Shake until the honey dissolves. Serve cold with a sprig of mint. Yields one serving.

This is a great source of vitamin C, fiber, potassium, and calcium.

locks and the key

Having thick, luxurious hair is an automatic guy magnet. According to studies men see long, thick healthy hair as a sign of fertility and health in a woman. Having a healthy scalp is essential to growing healthy hair. But having oily hair is a big turn off and hard to get rid of unless you know a few insider tricks. A way to heal the scalp, but get rid of the excess oil and sebum secretion is to exfoliate your head a couple of times a week.

exfoliate your head—a recipe for oily scalp problems

Our hair experts tell us that two times a week, after you shampoo, you should try this oil balancing treatment.

1   **egg and beat till foamy**
6   **tablespoons of natural yogurt.**

Apply this mixture to the scalp by partitioning hair and applying at the roots. Wait 15 minutes, then rinse and condition the hair as usual. This should gently slough off dead skin cells in a non-abrasive nourishing way.

bcb: extra helping

And while we are in the detoxing mode, let's do it from the inside out as well. You can't look your best and most beautiful if you have breakouts, bloating, headaches and puffiness. Most to the time that is due to a sluggish digestive system. That means it is time to DETOX. Dr. John Douillard, D.C., Ph.D., director of the LifeSpa Ayurveda center in Colorado, likens digestive problems to a clogged drain. "If you have too much mucus in your intestinal tract, the drains can get clogged, which creates toxicity in the lymph resulting in dilated blood vessels or headaches."

detox your digestive system with tea (like they do at a spa)

Dr. Douillard says that to lubricate your intestinal lining, drink teas with herbs like slippery elm, marshmallow, or licorice everyday. Traditional and medicinal Throat Coat is a great choice. To clean your lymphatic system even further take sips of hot water every 15 minutes for two weeks.

We feel cleaner, unclogged, less oily, and more radiant already!

brush your nails

So you've decided that home manicures and pedicures equal major savings. The problem is, you're not a professional, and the polish has this sneaky way of escaping your nail-bed and roaming over to your skin. It looks like a home job and you want it to look perfect. Never fear, because here's a quick fix that will make it look like you popped in for a mani-pedi at the local spa.

1   **teaspoon of any kind of oil (which can even include cooking oil or an essential oil)**
1   **old toothbrush**

Polish your nails without worrying that the polish might bleed a bit onto your skin. Before you apply any clear topcoat, let the polish dry completely.

Now, take the oil and spread it over your fingers where the polish has pulled an escape act. Take the old toothbrush and softly scrub the skin. All of the polish will come off your skin while it still stays on your nails.

This is a great tip for those who do home manicures because it's so hard to bend, polish, and make sure your tootsies are getting enough, but not too much, color. Don't worry about it now, polish away and then just remove the excess with the oil and the brush. The oil is also a great moisturizer. If you use scented oil then it will make your hands and feet smell yummy. Just don't put the toothbrush in the bathroom, because if you mistake it for your new one...yuck!

BCB EXPERT: KIM MATHESON, PRESIDENT, NATURAL RESOURCES SPA CONSULTING, INC.

Over here in Beauty Cookbook Land, we could adopt Kim Matheson. She's president of the world's most famous spa consulting company. She puts the top luxury spas on the map and helps determine their treatments and products. Kim also deals with a bevy of celeb clients, including Beyonce, Cindy Crawford, Paula Abdul, and even Sean Connery, plus skin-care pros, make-up artists, and hair gurus around the globe. She shared with us some amazing beauty tips, including how to create a real spa in your own bathroom. Kim should know. She sets up bliss for a living.

BCB: Okay, we have a big date on Friday night. What shouldn't we be doing on Tuesday, Wednesday, and Thursday to look our glowing best?

KM: No drinking, ladies! Say no to the sauce. No margaritas with your girlfriends. Alcohol dries out your skin and there is no cure for that one.

BCB: So what if we still look a little "tired" and the date is looming? Provide a 911 tip, we beg you!

KM: I like to pour some cool water in a bowl and fill it with a tea bag or two. Grab some large cotton balls or even a Kotex pad. Soak in the cool water. Now lie down for five or ten minutes to relax. Think positive thoughts and listen to beautiful music. This is a mini eye treatment that will get rid of your puff.

BCB: Tell us something impossibly French that we can do to look more gorgeous since you also set up spas in the city of love.

KM: French women know that real beauty doesn't end at the bottom of your neck. American women forget to take care of the whole body. French women will soak their nails in olive oil to have those beautiful cuticles and then put a little of the oil on the ends of their hair.

BCB: So many over-40 ladies have written to ask about redness in their skin. Any tips?

KM: Ladies who are red, stay away from the hot water when you wash. You should only wash in lukewarm water. Please don't drink or smoke, which just adds to redness. And do that old-fashioned trick of finishing a shower or facial wash with a cold-water blast to your face. It constricts the blood vessels, which makes you look less red. You will also want to nix spicy foods. By the way, the caffeine in your diet cola and coffee is making you much redder. I would suggest staying away from it.

Beauty Tip

It's amazing that you just made that onion-garlic potato salad for your family, but now your hands smell like a deli. Don't reach for the soap, but run to your bathroom and grab your mouthwash and a cotton ball. Rub your mouthwash-saturated cotton ball over your hands. The ethanol in the mouthwash will neutralize the garlic and onion. No more smelly hands!

BCB: Okay, not to ask questions just for ourselves, but...what about dry hair that just might be processed?

KM: You want to moisturize your scalp. You can even use

shea butter on your scalp. I'd suggest exfoliating a dry scalp gently with a soft wash cloth.

BCB: Now let's get to the fun part here. You set up luxury spas all over the globe. Can you give us a few tips when it comes to turning our own bathrooms into a haven of relaxation without it costing too much?

KM: First of all, think about what you love about a spa visit. Perhaps it's the full body scrub. Did you know that most spas spend next to nothing on the products they use for this scrub? Most of the time they have a big bag of salt in the back, which they mix with water and a little oil. Voila! It's a body scrub. You just add a little essential oil with a great smell like lavender or whatever you love. Sugar can also be used, but I prefer salt because it has more granules. You can make this mixture and use it all the time by just keeping a plastic bowl in your shower or near your bath. Add salt and water until you have a loose paste. Dilute with aromatherapy oils. Personally, I love Judith Jackson's natural oils. I love adding flowers, including rose petals, to this salt mix. Now, just use a cloth or a loofah and scrub your body from head to toe. It's natural, cheap, and you will be like silk.

BCB: What else should we buy for our bathroom spa?

KM: I love a big loofah or a wonderful sea sponge. I have a two-foot loofah and it's a real treat because you can do your entire back by yourself. If your skin is super-sensitive then try a nice dry body brush. The bristles will be soft, and you can simply brush dead skin off your entire body. Follow this treatment by slathering on a nice oil instead of lotion. Oil will make you softer. I'd also recommend candles, music, and a wonderful comfortable robe for your bathroom spa. Invest in a few fabulous towels that are just for you. These are not the towels you use all week long. Keep all of your goodies in a gorgeous basket that's also mobile. It will contain your brushes, mitts, finger and toe files, scrubs, and oils. It's great to have them in one place. Buy a gorgeous crystal glass that you will use for your water, tea, or even wine in the bathroom. I love a nice hand-crafted bar of soap that's pretty. Buy a little tray that's gorgeous for your toothbrush. Don't just plop it on the counter. The idea is that you will be spending time in here. That's what a spa experience is about…taking the time.

BCB: Tell us something that costs almost nothing, but is a nice treat.

KM: Take a drop of rosemary and place it in the middle of your hair brush. Your hair will smell great for a week. It might cost a few more dollars to buy a little wooden bench for your shower. I can't even begin to tell you how relaxing it is to sit on your bench with the steamy water pouring on you. It's better than therapy. I'd also buy bulbs for the bathroom that can be dimmed. You want this to be a soothing place.

BCB: Tell us why stars look so amazing and what tips we can steal from them.

KM: Stars get facials all of the time. If you can afford it, then I'd highly recommend it. They really do drink water and avoid the sun, plus they work out. Their diet is regulated and they take nutrition supplements. Come on! You better look good. As a regular person, you have to make the commitment to yourself to look and feel good. You can have a great diet and take vitamins, plus schedule a facial once in awhile if possible. Remember to eat and drink in moderation. Don't fall asleep with your makeup on because you will see and feel the difference. You also have to feel good about yourself and do good for others. All of this goes into being a beautiful person, which is reflected both inside and outside.

BCB: And if all else fails?

KM: Relax and find a good lover. Those two can't miss!

SEVENTH COURSE *a daily menu*

24-hour beauty blitz for free

6 am: Wake up. Brew a cup of java. Make scrambled eggs for the kids. Reserve one egg. Use the yolk on hair as a deep conditioner and the white from the egg on face as a mask.

6:20 am: Feed kids their egg breakfast and rinse off the egg white mask while they're eating. Stare at your tight pores and firm face. Put the egg yolk in your hair. Put your hair into a ponytail. Grab the coffee grinds and put them in a plastic container and bring them to the shower. Walk the kids to school, return home, and grab their hula hoop. Do 15 minutes of hula for a flatter tummy. Make a cup of coffee. Grab your natural sugar granules and a bottle of olive oil. Open the fridge and grab your odor-eating baking soda.

7 am: Head upstairs and jump into the shower with the coffee grinds, sugar, and olive oil. Remove the egg yolk from your scalp by washing, and revel in the shine and moisturizing effects. Then scrub away cellulite with the coffee grinds. This stimulates blood flow and helps pull out the toxins in hips, thighs, and tummies. Now, take your olive oil and add some sugar to exfoliate your elbows, knees, and legs. Start to see a glow.

Step out of the shower and mix some baking soda and Cetaphil at your bathroom sink. Exfoliate your face and then blow-dry your hair.

7:30 am: Head down to the laundry room to throw a new load in the washer. Pull the other clothes out of the dryer. Grab a Bounce sheet and run it down the shaft of your hair to eliminate the frizzies.

10 am: Neighbor calls and says she is coming over for a chat. You grab your kid's red magic marker from family room and dab it on your lips. You notice a zit forming and grab the Pepto Bismol to dry it out before dinner time. Just a dab will do.

12 pm: Friend comes over for a lunch of fruit salad. Reserve the extra blueberries for a late evening facial smoothie. Save one or two strawberries as a teeth whitener. (Yes, you can brush your teeth with them and they will remove plaque and brighten your smile.) Give your teeth a quick brush to get rid of the sugar from the strawberries. Use the leftover pineapple to give yourself a mani-pedi boost with the natural acid shaping up your cuticles.

2 pm: Baby is crying. Grab some Ambisol and put a dab on the baby's gums and another dab on your uni-brow. Pluck without pain. Grab baby's teething ring and put it in the freezer. Use it later as a natural way to de-puff eyes.

3 pm Kids home from school. A little playtime in the backyard on mini-trampoline. Eliminate 250 calories. A little sweaty? Grab some apple cider vinegar for under arm freshening. Feel stinky in your sneakers? Brew a little bit of black tea and put it in a low lipped dish. Soak your tootsies. Wow, does that feel good or what?

5 pm: Go out to the garden and grab some rose petals. Put a few in your bra for a natural perfume that will linger all evening. Grab a little coconut oil from the pantry to make your hair shine on the ends.

6 pm: Put aside a hot chocolate packet for later.

9 pm: Kids asleep. Run romantic bubble bath. Add the hot chocolate packet and invite hubby in for a skin-smoothing sexy soak. Sweet dreams.

EIGHTH COURSE *lifestyle recipes*

We're going to close the beauty kitchen for just a minute and share with you some fabulous lifestyle secrets that we found along the way. These are ideas for the rest of your life now that you're so gorgeous!

fast fix for sleep

You need your Zzzzz's. If you sleep at least six hours a day, but less than eight, you will live longer than if you sleep more or less than those figures, according to the Archives of General Psychiatry.

do you remember?

Don't throw away your orange peels. Keep fresh ones in a little cup next to your computer. One whiff of those peels will travel through your olfactory system and will stimulate your brain's limbic system or memory center. It will take just one second to have a memory jolt.

owie no more

You or your little ones got a cut or scrape, so you put that big ol' bandage on. Now, since the medical emergency is over, you want to go out and don't want to have the unsightly big cover, but *ouccch!*—how to peel it off? We know a secret cure. Simply grab a bottle of your hair conditioner from the shower and smooth a dime size amount on the sticky strip. Let it sit for one minute and then peel off. The conditioner's oils will break down the adhesives that bond the dressing to the skin, so it will come of easily and gently. Now, you're ready for your event, owie-free.

eye opening

Please stop adding drops of water to your favorite eye shadow as a way to turn it into a liner. This is a fabulous way of creating a bacteria nightmare when the water interacts with the rest of the shadow, which then can get moldy as it dries out. If you want to try this look, simply wet your cosmetics brush with a few eye drops. These are made from sterile materials and won't allow bacteria to grow in your shadows.

aloe allergy remedy

Allergies, puffiness, and sneezing making you look red and swollen or making you tired and cranky? We have just the trick if you suffer from pollen, irritants, and allergens. Forget all those high prices and medicated treatments. The nose has blood vessels and nerves, so a way to calm the itching and sneezing is to grab a Q-tip, put a drop of Aloe Vera gel on it, and rub the inside of your nose with it. The natural healing gel will soothe and calm the interior and calm your face and breathing—you will not only feel your best, but you will look better too!

for your aching tootsies: not-so-natural high

If your new high heels are killing you in certain spots then find that medical tape that's probably in a kitchen drawer. Put a strip of the strong tape over the areas before they blister. Instant avoidance from future pain from the pumps!

for your posture: bewitched

For those rounded shoulders which don't look good on the beach (or anywhere), just grab a kitchen broom, stand up straight, hold the broomstick behind your back and under your butt, with your arms straight, your hands shoulder-width apart, and your palms facing out. Slowly, lift the bar behind your back as high as you can. Don't lift the shoulders but bring the shoulder blades together behind your back. Hold for ten seconds. This will straighten out your posture pronto.

for your clothes: fast fix for panty hose horrors

Use your empty paper towel holders to keep your panty hose from getting runs while they're in your sock drawer. Just cut the paper towel tubes in half, gently place hose inside of them and even write the color and make of the hose on the outside for quick morning hose pick-ups.

fast fix for faded clothes

Want to dazzle with your duds? The answer should be "yes," because we certainly don't think you should be limited in your dazzle powers. We want to help your clothes look better, too. Here's a quick recipe to keep your outfits looking great and the colors in them bright, strong, and vibrant all year long. For greens, yellows, and pinks.

1   teaspoon of black pepper

Put these garments in your washer and set to a coldwater load. Add the teaspoon of black pepper. The piperine in the pepper will keep your colors from draining and fading. A bonus is this trick will also help stop these vibrant colors from running in the wash.

for your lovely home: orange you glad we told you these things?

We love taking a few slices of oranges and rubbing them on our faces for a quick luminosity boost of vitamin C, but this magic fruit is also good for many tasks around your house, including getting rid of bugs. If you have an area where pesky bugs seem to reappear, and even the exterminator can't figure it out, then grate a few orange peels and sprinkle them in the area. Ants and flies hate the smell of oranges and will flee.

grapefruit as a cheap room spray

Studies show that the scent of grapefruit on your body makes others believe that you are years younger than your real age. Another great use of an actual grapefruit is to take those rinds that usually hit the Hefty bag and put them in the bottom of a spray bottle that you fill with water. Instead of expensive room sprays, your homemade fresh and tart smell is great for a booster or in smell challenged areas like the garbage can or near where the dog sleeps. You can even put a few drops on your showerhead for an amazingly fresh bathroom smell that will help wake you up in the morning with its crisp, light scent.

going bananas

Grab those empty banana peels and use them to shine your favorite leather products, including good shoes and even purses. The oil in the peels will moisturize your leather without staining it, while the potassium located in the peels will give your leather a little extra protection against scratching.

for your health: flu, who?

None of us can afford to be sick these days because we can't afford to take days off work or hire a babysitter to cope with kids who need our attention. Bottom line is, we just can't fit the flu into our schedules! One insider tip to avoid the flu while keeping up with your hectic lifestyle is to take an olive leaf capsule every day. Oh, and wash your hands often, too, to get rid of germs. (Note to pregnant and nursing women: Make sure you check with your physician before you use these or any of our remedies or other recommendations in our book!)

no oil, just vinegar

This isn't a diet book, but we have come across a few kitchen diet secrets that are too good, so we must share. Scientists in Sweden have found that if you're eating a high carb meal make sure to have 2 tablespoons of vinegar with it. It's easy if you have a salad with oil and vinegar, but make sure you use enough vinegar. Why? This study found that those two measly teaspoons of vinegar lowered your blood sugar by 23 percent. An added boost is that vinegar is full of antioxidants.

any way you slice it

So many models, celebrities, and very slim women we have talked to over the years all swear by one, easy, at-home, from-your-kitchen trick to start their day. It's just your basic drink of fresh lemon with water. Sure, you've heard this before, but perhaps you don't know the science behind it. Lemon actually cleanses your liver and thus turns your system into the fat-burning machine it was designed to be for you. Quite often, one of the reasons the body clings to extra weight is that you might have an overstressed or toxic liver. This drink will help kick-start your system again.

Just take the juice of one-half of a freshly squeezed organic lemon and add it to six ounces of warm water. Mix, or even put in the blender with some ice, if you like it cold. Drink the mixture and wait 30 minutes before eating or drinking anything else.

for your mental health

- **Mint Makeover**: If you're feeling an afternoon low, keep something minty around your work or home. Research indicates that a quick smell of this invigorating scent actually revs up your brain activity. One or two whiffs and you will feel alert again and raring to go!

- **Attitude Adjuster**: One of the fastest and almost zero-cost ways to improve your mood is to reach for the tube—and we don't mean the television. Yes, mental health pros tell us that the simple act of putting on lipstick can improve your mood. Staring at your new beautiful self in the mirror can't hurt either!

SIDE-DISHING WITH KYM AND CINDY

Kym: Let's start at the beginning. I was seven pounds, six ounces at birth, and bald until I was two. White hair and bald! White hair you couldn't see! This was technically the only time in my life I wasn't worried about my hair or trying to get a blow out. Zero to three. I was good!

Cindy: I was five pounds when I was born. It was the thinnest I've ever been in my life. Oh, and I was born with almost no hair. My mom used to tape a bow to the top of my head. Now it would be considered child abuse because I think she had to use duct tape to make it stick. It was historically the first time I used a product.

Kym: It was probably non-toxic glue.

Cindy: Probably. I did progress to the middle school years where I had delusions I could have Marsha Brady hair. It was my first crushing hair disappointment because Marsha didn't have curly, brown, frizzy, Midwestern hair. Her hair was California, professionally done, stick-straight. Her hair was Brady and mine was perpetually wind-blown, partially because I lived in the Windy City of Chicago, and partially because I don't think my hair knew it was required for life to look like my favorite stars of both the big and small screens. Already, I was setting myself up for major disappointment.

Kym: I had really thick, naturally wavy hair, too. It didn't help that my mother shaved my head in a sink and then put Nice and Easy blonde dye on it. It went from white blonde to a dirty pre-teen blonde. What can you say? My mom was Miss Scotland and thought she had another Miss Scotland in the making, even though we lived in Michigan. I was like, "Mom, we live 5,000 miles away from Scotland and I'm not going to win." And all that dye made my hair frizz, so my teenage years were over-processed and naturally wavy. By the way, I also thought I was Marsha Brady, but I looked like Jan. And who wanted to be Jan? She had the bangs that curled.

Cindy: Jan, we love you, but we don't want to be you.... But we digress. Finally, I went to Connie, my mom's hairdresser. I couldn't bring myself to say that I wanted Farrah Fawcett hair when I was in eighth grade. So I bought a hairstyling magazine and memorized the instructions of the Farrah cut, which wasn't easy because they were complicated. I went into the suburban salon and said in my most professional voice, "I want graduated layers that begin six inches from my crown and feather lightly about five inches past my chin." Connie looked at me like I was nuts and gave me her basic cut that she gave to everyone who sat in her chair. She gave me Dorothy Hamill hair! How could you go from Farrah to Dorothy? It was that very day that I learned the cruelty of hairdressers. She had my teenage fate in her hands. I remember leaving there crying and thinking, "No offense, Dorothy. You're a great athlete, but I want Jill Monroe from *Charlie's Angels* and not some short, bubbly ice skater's hair." I mean, I couldn't even roller skate in those days. It was so wrong.

Kym: I feel your pain. I remember my first prom, which was a church prom. God forbid I go to a real one. I was about 14 and liked this boy named Larry who was a bit older. Of course, I was also going to look like Farrah and have Farrah hair even if it killed me. So, I went to my mother for some help and we rolled my hair into sausage curls. It wasn't Farrah, but some sort of pasta hair that belonged on the menu of an Italian restaurant. But Larry liked it, so I could breathe a sigh of relief.

Cindy: Even worse was the fact that my neighbor was the Clinique makeup woman. Before my first big school dance, she came over for a makeover and I should have known this would be a disaster. This was the same woman who regularly made up her child to look like Dorothy in *The Wizard of Oz*. Oh, her child was a boy—and it wasn't even Halloween. I just remember she had a plastic bucket filled with little samples and she got to work with this serious, dangerous glint in her eyes. It was like we were doing open-heart surgery.

When it was done, I had tons of eye-shadow on in deep purples, heavily lined eyes, and lashes that went from my bedroom to the front door. Mortifying! I looked like the only 26-year-old in seventh grade. My history teacher thought I was his date.

Kym: Enough hair. Now, let's get to skin.

Cindy: Really. Is this necessary?

Kym: Absolutely. My skin horror was the light up, three-way mirror that I purchased as a teenager and put on my desk. I would put full makeup on in seventh grade in a dark bedroom. When I left for school, I looked like I was going to a disco club. I would layer the makeup on, but I thought it looked beautiful. Can you say *I work the streets*?

Cindy: Skin was another issue for me, too. I would lay out on my grassy, bug-filled Midwestern expanse of lawn and put iodine and oil over my entire body and then cook out there while reading the classics...*People*, *US Weekly*, *USA Today*. And later, I wondered and worried why someone with fair skin was so red after five or six hours in the sun. Imagine!

Kym: By the way, at least you didn't do what I did for nutrition. Someone told me in those days that baby food could be a great diet. So, I'd get jars of fruit dessert and run out the door with my mom chasing me with toast and eggs. Miss Sweden could run very fast, but I could go faster. I didn't want those carbs from the toast. For lunch, I'd have a Hostess blueberry pie, solid sugar and pastry with four blueberries in it. Then I'd have yogurt with tons of sugar. At night, I'd count my calories for dinner. Four bites of whatever they were having. Then I was full. On weekends, my girlfriend Kim and I would go buy a 24-ounce bottle of Tab with zero calories. Tab was the diet for Saturday because I was saving calories, plus it was the cool drink of the day. If you came up with the worst diet for your teenage skin, I could write that book.

Cindy: The colder the Tab, the better, and I loved the little pink cans. I remember dessert being very important in those days—and I had fine taste buds. I did the Hostess chocolate cupcakes with the little swirl down the middle. I think my local store kept them for about a year or two, which is why the cake part was almost a chalky dust that blew away entirely upon opening. But it still tasted great with a cold Tab because I figured that you always needed diet, chemically filled soda, with your desserts. Come on! If you're having a 500-calorie treat, you certainly couldn't afford the extra drink calories. Later, I knew that if you just ate the peel of frosting, you would be saving additional calories. Can you even imagine how that sugar wreaked havoc on my teenage skin? It's funny how, in those days, we unknowingly did everything we could to destroy the beauty we would spend the rest of our lives chasing after.

THE LATER YEARS

Cindy: Now we sail into our twenties.

Kym: I was anchoring the news in upstate Michigan. It was part of my job to put on a lot of makeup and stand in front the cameras. I thought the amount of makeup I put on in seventh grade was just right for the camera. But soon I began to see how it was affecting my skin. Why was I still having breakouts in my twenties? Of course, sitting under hot lights with caked-on foundation embedded in every pore didn't help. And carrying equipment through the woods of northern Michigan was really drying for my skin.

Cindy: In Chicago, I was working as a newspaper reporter. Running around a city that's often 10 degrees below zero in the winter was really drying. But at least I had youth on my side…not to mention running eyes from the cold. So attractive. Oh, I washed my face with a bar of Ivory soap at night. The horror!

Kym: Now, we know that strong soaps and the wrong astringent can actually destroy your skin. Who knew at the time?

Cindy: I used rubbing alcohol as an astringent. I would take cotton balls filled with rubbing alcohol, stuff that made your eyes really water, and put it on any oily spots. You could use that stuff to make beef jerky and it was my daily beauty routine. This time youth and lack of knowledge wasn't on my side.

Kym: Now, we're mature enough to have a lot of knowledge. We're not going to sit in the sun with album covers directing more rays our way or slather on the baby oil. We're not going to skip washing at night or go a day without moisturizer.

Cindy: We're not going to get a department store perm!

Kym: No! You didn't!

Cindy: I won't mention the store, but it was frightening. After you signed five legal papers that exonerated them from all charges, they took you into this back room filled with mops, cleaning equipment, and one lone hairdresser chair that looked like the place they took Michael Clarke Duncan in *The Green Mile*. I think the hairdresser swept up the automotive aisles while my perm percolated. I went from naturally straight to crazy curly/frizzy. I went home and washed the perm with hardcore Prell, which just made it worse. Think Barbara in *A Star Is Born*.

TURNING 40

Kym: I have to admit that I was the lone holdout in that I loved turning 40. I just had a baby and my career was going really well. My husband, Jerry Douglas, was at the height of his fame on the *Young and the Restless*. I refused to buy into thinking I was over the hill. Everyone was saying that 40 was the new 30. I didn't mind hitting the number. I did begin to realize that I should really look at all the additives, chemicals, and synthetics in my diet and skin care routines.

Cindy: It seems like a major milestone to me in many ways, hitting the big 4-*oh*. Something clicked on the skin care front and I knew I had to start paying serious attention. Awareness is key and I began to seek knowledge in how to take care of my skin without any shots or cutting because I'm such a wuss about that kind of thing. I also began to learn how you really need products with no chemicals in them.

Kym: Knowledge is power. Learning about chemicals and additives gave us the blueprint of where we wanted to go and how to look our best. But it's our personal best. It's not about having Farrah's hair anymore or Kelly Ripa's hair color. It's about being the best we can be.

Cindy: Well, it's a little about having Jennifer Aniston's hair color. I have to be honest here. But the point is, we've also spent so much money on products over the years that it's time to stop and re-evaluate how to get the best skin and hair without breaking the bank, or buying so many products that our bathrooms look like department store cosmetics counters. I got to the point where I couldn't even find my toothbrush anymore. But that damn Ivory soap was still there from the '70s.

Kym: At age 45, I said, "Wait a minute. I'm literally subsidizing the cosmetic companies of the world. I have a house to pay for and a life that comes before buying these products." It's silly to pay $200 for a cream when I can make one in my kitchen. Why would I want to spend big dollars on a tiny jar of eye cream when there were natural ingredients that were so much healthier?

Cindy: Now, we know that these lotions and potions are mostly just cheap lotions and a few ingredients that we tell you how to use in this book. The funny thing is, everyone wants to do what the celebs are doing. But most celebs are usually worried about money and they're not spending $350 on eye creams.

Kym: Simple really is the best. You just have to be diligent about your routine and disciplined about it.

Cindy: We learned that the best beauty things in life are pretty close to free and they're in your kitchen.

Kym: Women can look so beautiful just using natural ingredients that are pure and that your skin easily absorbs. And now we don't have to go to Neiman's and toss the keys at the valet. We sit at home and let our elbows soak in grapefruits and put avocado on our hair.

Cindy: I love the egg-white facial, and I use those pineapple rings to create great cuticles. Forget expensive manicures, although it does look like I have two a week. My dogs like the leftover pineapple rings, too. They don't use it on their nails, but they do scarf them down.

Kym: The hot chocolate bath is beyond. My husband thinks I'm nuts, but he likes the champagne bath.

Cindy: But I still want Farrah hair. Just for one day. Please. No offense, Dorothy Hamill, but some dreams will never go out of style.

Kym: I want the hair, but I'm not wearing the red one-piece suit!

Cindy: I will if you will.

Kym: That's our next book.

If you have any great beauty recipes, please send them to us at www.hollywoodbeautylift.com or www.kymdouglas.com

Beauty and blessings,

Kym and Cindy

appendix

SNEAKY WAYS TO MAKE YOUR GUY LOOK SEXIER

Shhhhhhh. Keep these following pages top secret, ladies. We know you might be a bit bothered by your mate's…um…hygiene habits—or maybe even the toll aging has taken on him. But remember, there is nothing sexy about nagging your man to start a beauty regime. He will probably laugh, ignore you, and grab the remote control and turn to ESPN. The key here is to do beauty treatments on your man without him ever knowing what you're doing. Sneaky? Yes. Necessary? Maybe.

We have a few never-fail tricks that you can sneak into your own house. Good luck, Jane Bond.

male hair loss recipe

His hair is not the thick mat it used to be. But don't despair. Just add two tablespoons of ground flaxseed to his daily diet (in oatmeal, yogurt, stew, orange juice, or salad). This will slow the fallout by helping to balance the high levels of hormones, which is what's behind the hair loss.

thinning hair rescue

Use one tablespoon of chopped basil and ¼ cup of olive oil that you mix together. Apply to his scalp. Do this by insisting you're going to give him a sexy bathroom spa treatment. The basil promotes growth because it stimulates the scalp. You can even heat the basil and oil mix in the microwave for 30 seconds, let cool, and then apply to his scalp. Kiss him profusely because you need to leave this on for 15 minutes. Now, suggest a shower because you need to shampoo it out.

snowy men

So your guy has dandruff? We're sorry, but that's a bit gross and it has to stop. Suggest that he rub a bit of aloe vera gel into his scalp—every day. Ask him to leave it on for a few minutes (maybe five) and then shower. He can then shampoo it out. Using lime juice to wash his hair is another great trick to get rid of the flakes.

Beauty Tip

If he has athlete's foot, take one tablespoon of baking soda and add a few drops of water. Have him work the paste between his toes. Let this set for ten minutes. Then rinse and powder with cornstarch.

not-so-happy feet

It's great that your husband is living in the gym and created that six-pack ab look, but his feet…*PU*. If your mate is stinking up the house, there is a simple solution. Take four tea bags and put them in a quart of boiling water, let cool, and then tell your guy that you're going to give him a very sexy foot massage. It will feel good on his tootsies, but it will also get rid of that funky smell. When he's done, make sure he allows his feet to air dry completely, and do not rinse. Why? The tannin in the tea is a natural drying agent and will de-skunk even the most putrid piggies. By the way, the tea also keeps your pores dry, which will also help stop perspiration.

odor eaters

First, some medical knowledge.

Did you know that sweat actually has no smell? It's the bacteria on your skin that creates that foul-smelling BO. A quick, natural, and easy way to solve the BO issue is with apple cider vinegar, and according to our sources, it's no "Secret" (forgive the pun) that it actually works better

Beauty Tip

Just in case you are not a tea drinker, and have the foot-odor issue, then there is one other cure we have for you. Tea Tree Oil has antifungal and antiseptic properties, which makes it the perfect answer to smelly tootsies. Rub your feet with a few drops every day after your shower.

Beauty Tip

If your man has ragged cuticles and jagged nails, you might have to sneak in a quick home manicure. Don't get out the girlie manicure stuff that will make him run for the backyard and a cold beer. Just casually grab a paper clip and use it to push back his cuticles. Then sneak in a matchbook. No, you're not going to light some candles and pray that he was more into grooming. You'll simply use the strike strip on the matchbook to shape and file his broken nails.

than deodorant! The apple cider vinegar lowers your skin's pH level, which kills odor-causing bacteria. So, if you want to cut back on high-priced underarm deodorant and antiperspirants, just soak a cotton ball in vinegar and apply generously to your under arms daily. The vinegar smell will dissipate, leaving you smelling beautifully sweet, fresh, and odor free.

bushman be gone

Bushy eyebrows are back, but sometimes your guy gets too hairy and goes from sexy to an unappealing wild-man look. We know he won't go to an eyebrow stylist (just for chicks), but how about just grabbing your Chapstick, ladies. Sweep some quickly over his arches to keep the unruly brow hairs in perfect place.

index

acknowledgments

FROM KYM

Firstly, nothing is possible without the Lord at the helm of my life, so all honor goes to Like the famous ninety-year-old preacher Billy Graham said in a recent speech, "Life without God is like an unsharpened pencil—it has no point."

To my loving, beautiful, and always glamorous mother, Barbara Bankier. Thank you for sparking the desire in me to want to be beautiful inside and out at a very young age.

To the hero and rock of my life—my father, John Bankier. Never has there been a more successful, honorable, spiritual, and righteous man to walk this earth than the man I am blessed to have as my father: John Barton Bankier. You are my everything, and I stand in awe of your example to me of what it truly is to be a good, good person. You taught me, Dad, to do what is right, even when no one else is looking!

To my other rock, and my love—my husband, Jerry Douglas. As an actor on *The Young and the Restless*, still his day job, he was my first interview out of college. I interviewed him, he asked me out to dinner, we got married. Jerry, you let me fly, soar, run, and rest in the security of your love and support of all my dreams. I could have done none of this without your strong and supportive arms around me.

To the angel of my life, my only son, Hunter William Douglas. You inspire me. You are my miracle child. I want to be like you when I grow up! You are wise beyond your years, kind, honest, true to yourself, and a young man I truly admire.

To my publisher, David Dunham, who found me, reached out to me, believed we could make this project happen, said he would make it happen, and then made it happen. David, you do what you say and say what you do. You give the best of yourself to your work and expect the same from those you work with. You are pure perfection, Mr. Dunham! It has been a delight to work with you and I hope (know!) we have many more best-sellers in our future together!

To Emily Prather, the brilliant editor who so quickly and graciously jumped on board to edit, clean, and take this work from 0 to 10 in just a few weeks!! Whew.

To my business partner and manager, Debi Baer...say whaaat? If I hadn't found you, it would be like Lucy not having Ethel, Oprah not having Gayle, Lavern not having Shirley. We laugh, we cry, we mother, we wife, we shop...but in truth we make our dreams a reality every single day! I could not do it without you and wouldn't want to. You make the journey so much sweeter and more fun.

To *The Ellen DeGeneres Show* and Warner Brothers who have been more than wonderful to me—the greatest people in the world to work for. Ellen is, well, how do I describe a woman who lets me walk on her show, opens her arms and her heart, and just lets me do my thing? She is immensely talented, generous to a fault, and kinder to me than anyone in Hollywood has ever, ever been. I love you, Ellen, and will forever be grateful to you.

And to Matthew Wright, the producer of all producers. Your

creativity and genius is what makes the magic happen for me in my segments on *Ellen*. You found me, you brought me to *The Ellen DeGeneres Show*, and you took a risk on me—all because of the vision and belief you had in me. I will forever love and adore you. You are the baby brother I never had.

Because of the executive producing team of the gorgeous and witty Andy Lassner, the handsome and charming Ed Glavin, and the intelligent and lovely Mary Connelly, I get the great honor to appear again and again on *The Ellen DeGeneres Show*. These brilliant and talented people make magic everyday for all of us to enjoy. They are the gate keepers who entertain millions, and I get to work with them. I am one lucky girl with a lot of maple syrup on her hair!

Good Day LA Fox KTTV is the #1 rated morning show in Southern California, and I have been blessed to work there for over fifteen years. A big thank-you to Hose Rios, the fabulous and talented news director there who is one of the kindest, warmest, and smartest men I have ever met. And, Hose, your precious daughter, Sarafina, is an angel.

I would also like to thank my dear friend and the executive producer of *Good Day LA*, Lisa Kridos, who has been my hero and guide for over fifteen years in the business. She is tall, beautiful, smart, and strong, and she says what she feels—all qualities I need in my life and in my business. My FOX senior executive producer, Josh Kaplan, is a gem. He is a man who is talented, powerful yet gentle, funny, and always kind to all. That is a truly successful man! Nicole Prentice is such a special person and friend, she produces my segments on GDLA with such sweetness and talent, all the while being pregnant. Nicole, you are kind and gentle and such a wonderful person, and your girls are so blessed to have you as their mom. And I am blessed to have you as my producer.

A huge thank-you to General Manager, Kevin Hale, who is

a wonderful and supportive friend and boss. And to the talented morning news show team I'm privileged to work with: Jillian Barberie Reynolds, you are a "girl's girl" who has been sweet, supportive, and kind to me since day one. Jillian loves to promote others and see them succeed. You're a doll, Jill. Dorothy Lucey is a soul sister. We share so many of the same things and I love to shop, gossip, and go to church with her, but not necessarily in that order. LOL.

Steve Edwards "I hate you!" (Not really.) Steve and I have worked together for over fifteen years. He hates me but he likes my husband so I guess that is why I am still on the show. We have a love/ hate relationship. I hate that Steve teases me and Steve loves to tease me all the more. He is a great guy, and we have such fun together. But he always introduces me on camera as Jerry Douglas' wife!

To my producer, Lisa Bernstein, who really did discover me long ago and far away on a show called *Home & Family*. Lisa, we have worked together so long I feel like you truly are my home and my family.

To my writing partner, life-time friend, and confidante, Cindy Pearlman. Cindy, we have had a fabulous, glamorous ride together. We see it, we say it, and we write it. Writing four books with you has been the dream of my life. I love what we put down on paper and how we empower and inspire women and men. Mostly, I love how we make them laugh because we laugh at ourselves.

Also to my wonderful agents at Kaplan/Stahler Agency, the dynamic Lisa Pollack and fabulous Sean Zeid, thank you for all of your great work.

FROM CINDY

This book would not have been possible without the vision of publishing genius, David Dunham. David, meeting you this year has been a great joy. Thank you for your outstanding creativity, commitment to excellence and nothing less, and for being there every step of the way. I'm looking forward to what 2010 will bring.

Thanks to Emily Prather. From the first moment we talked, I knew that you would make this book great—and you did. Thank you for using your editorial abilities to give these pages a beauty makeover!

Thanks always to my partner in beauty crime, co-writer, and friend, Kym Douglas. We decided last year to reinvent our beauty books and this is the result. Kym, thank you for your dedication, creativity, and the amazing ways you promote these books. This has been a great partnership and friendship. There is no recipe in this book that matches your joy, beauty, commitment, and talent. I wish you only the best for 2010.

Thank you to Richard Abate for your belief in me, amazing guidance over the years, and neverending support for my dream projects. It is my honor, joy, and pleasure to work with you. This is the year.

Endless thanks to the great editors in my life. Thanks to John Barron, Amanda Barrett, Miriam Di Nunzio, Darel Jevens, and Laura Emerick at the *Chicago Sun-Times* for your many years of wonderful friendship and support. Thanks to the amazing editor, Gayden Wren, at *The New York Times* syndicate.

To Joy, Sally, and Vickie, three of the best friends a girl could be lucky enough to have in life.

To G. Pelliteri, thank you from the bottom of my heart for your amazing work with me this year. You're a great friend and teacher.

Thanks to my brother and attorney, Gavin M. Pearlman, for always looking out for my best interests and for loving me unconditionally. Love to Jill, Reid, Cade, and Wylie. Thanks and love to Richard and Cheryl Pearlman, Jason, Kim, Craig, Beth, Nathan, Max, and Phoebe.

Thanks to my father, Paul Pearlman, for a lifetime of support and love.

To Ron. The past. The present. The future. With love.